T0354646

THE

UNDERGROUND

CULTURE

OF

GOVERNMENT

HOUSING

AN INTROSPECTIVE LOOK INTO
A FASCINATING SUBCULTURE

ALLAN LEE JAMES

authorHOUSE®

AuthorHouse™
1663 Liberty Drive
Bloomington, IN 47403
www.authorhouse.com
Phone: 833-262-8899

© 2021 Allan Lee James. All rights reserved.

No part of this book may be reproduced, stored in a retrieval system, or transmitted by any means without the written permission of the author.

Published by AuthorHouse   06/11/2021

ISBN: 978-1-6655-2907-5 (sc)
ISBN: 978-1-6655-2906-8 (hc)
ISBN: 978-1-6655-2905-1 (e)

Library of Congress Control Number: 2021911958

Print information available on the last page.

Any people depicted in stock imagery provided by Getty Images are models, and such images are being used for illustrative purposes only. Certain stock imagery © Getty Images.

This book is printed on acid-free paper.

Because of the dynamic nature of the Internet, any web addresses or links contained in this book may have changed since publication and may no longer be valid. The views expressed in this work are solely those of the author and do not necessarily reflect the views of the publisher, and the publisher hereby disclaims any responsibility for them.

"An introspective look at the *Underground Culture* of Government Housing"

This book is a first-hand account of experiences through the eyes of many employees who dedicate their talents to the everyday tasks of procuring clean, safe, Government housing for families and individuals.

When I received the position of Regional Maintenance Technician, I was excited to become a member of a team that helped people in need of affordable housing. As an employee of one of the largest taxpayer backed housing companies in America, however, over the years, I witnessed and compiled many accounts of sociological behaviors that I found troubling and confusing.

This book reflects the accounts of the attitudes and actions of many of the tenants we were tasked to aid -specifically with regards to safe and comfortable housing. It is also a direct look at the government assistance provided and the undeniable coddling these agencies demand thru every aspect of Government housing

I walked into a situation where I was immediately trained to perform my responsibilities with the attitude towards the tenants that they were all unfortunate individuals and families that were entitled to free or almost free housing. Basically, I was told that the American taxpayer covered the bills for these unfortunate people and I was instructed and that I had to respect and support this mission.

I immediately realized this request was going to be a difficult for me. Being in my late 50's age wise, I possessed an innate sense at a very young age that I was responsible for myself. That invariably meant I had to WORK to earn money to take care of my responsibilities

I am going to present my background to provide the reader with an introspective look on why this subject matter is passionate to me and how, as a society working together, we can solve some of the problems facing what I call the "underground culture of government housing."

CONTENTS

OVERVIEW OF WORK ETHIC

My "work ethic" background started when I was a ten-year-old growing up in a relatively small community of a population of 65,000. My parents worked very hard to afford us food, shelter, and clothing. They were of the Catholic faith and believed in "building the kingdom of God" which in turn gave me many siblings. My mother waitressed, and my father hauled salt to customers that had water softeners. They worked many hard hours for the family and NEVER complained.

As a family consisting of seven children, we had enough to eat and always had shelter. I noticed at a young age that my parents were the type that wanted to ensure success. I used their model of work as an example to obtain the things necessary to survive and then thrive in this world.

With that example, I wanted material things for myself. So I sat down and wrote in an old leftover notebook some ideas to earn money. Jobs that would be conducive to a ten-year-old. With my earnings, my first acquisition was going to be a round, green snow saucer! This saucer was sold at a store back in the late 60's called Prange Way. The store was located across town about five miles from our home. My plan was to hand out fliers, hand-made, to potential customers in our neighborhood describing my snow-shoveling business. (Now I was only ten years old and maybe looked seven, but I was fairly good at sales and successfully obtained several accounts. Now all I had to do was wait for it to snow).

After the first snow fall, I received several calls for snow removal at these peoples' homes. My customers were usually elderly people or customers without children of their own. So they had no one who was able to shovel for them. I worked all day as fast as I could shoveling driveways and sidewalks. I made enough money to buy that saucer I had set out to do. The only problem for me was getting to Prange Way five miles across town. My parents were too busy to take me and had enough problems and challenges taking care of my siblings.

So early on I learned that when there was a problem, there invariably was a solution. Even at a young age, I was going to figure out how to get that saucer. It had just snowed and NOW was the time to ACT!

I knew I couldn't ride my sister's bike all the way across town on the slushy streets and sidewalks, so I put my sloppy heavy boots on and decided I could run all the way there and back no matter how hard or tiring it would be. I finally had the cash and was motivated to reap the benefits of my hard work. Nothing would deny me of that.

When I entered the store, I received some odd looks from the employees. I guess they were wondering where my parents were. Remember, I was a ten-year-old that looked (at best) seven. I walked around to find where the saucers were displayed and when I discovered where they were, it was like I had just followed a great big beautiful rainbow and found the pot of gold! I was in pure jubilation! I bought that saucer with a huge smile on my face and proceeded to run all the way back home. I had achieved my goal. At that moment, I knew there was nothing in this world within reason that was not attainable with a plan, a goal, and hard work.

SO WHY AM I TELLING THIS STORY?

This story serves as an anecdote of my 'mind set' of what I believed to be normal behavior to achieve my goals. When I began working in government housing, I wanted to keep an open mind why these tenants were in housing. How did they get there and how could I fully understand how they strayed from what I understood was the norm.

It is my goal that these personal accounts serve as a wake up call for young children to examine the history of government housing in hopes the patterns would stop repeating.

MY FIRST DAY

Fast forward to 2011 when I received a phone call inquiring if I would be interested in working in the maintenance division for a private company that owned many properties around the United States. These government subsidized properties housed seniors and families and singles.

When the call came at that point in my career, I had retired from managing restaurants. I had amassed my own rental properties encompassing 42 tenants that I was personally responsible for. However, given my work ethic, I was looking for something to do in tandem with owning/managing my own properties. I thought this new job would be an easy way to help fill up my week considering I already had a manager for my own properties. Looking back, I had no idea what I was getting myself into.

The following information taken from the Institute of Research on Poverty, University of Wisconsin-Madison, National Taxpayers Union (NTU) and masslegalhelp.org:

CHAPTER 1

Public and/or Subsidized Housing

Public housing was established to provide decent and safe rental housing for eligible low-income families, the elderly, and persons with disabilities. Public housing comes in all different sizes and types, from scattered single-family houses to high-rise apartments for elderly families.

There are approximately 1.2 million households living in public housing units, managed by 3,300 Has (housing authorities). The U.S. Department of Housing and Urban Development (HUD) administers Federal aid to local housing agencies (HAs) that manage the housing for low-income residents at rents they can afford. HUD furnishes technical and professional assistance in planning, developing and managing these developments.

Who is eligible?

Public housing is limited to low-income families and individuals. An HA determines your eligibility based on: 1) Annual income; 2) whether you qualify as elderly, a person with disability, or as a family; and 3) U.S. citizenship or immigration status. If you are eligible, the HA will check your references to make sure you and your family will be good tenants. Has will deny admission to any applicant whose habits and practices may be expected to have detrimental effect on other tenants or on the project's environment.

Who owns public housing properties?

If you live in public housing, the housing authority owns the building and is your landlord. In a few cases, a private company may manage the building for the housing authority or may be part of the ownership, but the building is still controlled by the housing authority.

Who owns subsidized housing properties?

If you live in subsidized housing, the housing authority is not your landlord. Subsidized housing is owned and operated by private owners who receive subsidies in exchange for renting to low- and moderate income people. Owners may be individual landlords or for-profit or non-profit corporations.

In practice, these housing programs in most cases, will pay the balance of a rent payment that exceeds 30% of a renter's monthly income. Example: if a tenant earns $1000.00 a month, that tenants responsible rent is $300.00 per month. Moreover, if a tenant has zero income, that tenants responsible rent is 0.00 for that month. Also, in almost every case, heat and water is included with separate vouchers for electric bills. Note: the American taxpayer fits the bill for **all** vouchers.

These voucher programs serve nearly 2 million low-income families in the United States. For society as a whole, total benefits range from about $7,700 to $9,600 per year per tenant. The bulk of the benefits are experienced by voucher recipients, while other members of society bear the bulk of the costs. In other words – the American taxpayer. In other words, taxpayers are not only being forced to subsidize efforts which ensure a steady stream of taxpayer dollars will continue to be poured into the program, even as the federal government regularly runs an annual deficit of over **$1 trillion** dollars.

DAY ONE- Description of My First Property

I interviewed with the district manager and she hired me on the spot. On my first day, I was given keys to the property and was on my own. I decided to explore the compound and try and figure out what keys fit all the different locks, doors and storage areas. To my surprise, the place was in complete disarray.

I discovered six buildings consisting of twelve townhouses each and four buildings of sixteen apartments each. The townhouses had three floors consisting of a full basement, first floor and second floor. These townhouses offered three bedrooms, one and a half bathrooms and a kitchen fully equipped with appliances and garbage disposals. The two apartment buildings are one level apartments with two bedrooms and equipped with the same amenities as the townhouses. There is storage space provided in a common basement area for each individual apartment and washers/dryers in a laundry room.

In walking around the grounds, which was quite large, I noticed a picnic area supplied with grills, picnic tables and garbage cans. There is a children's playground, two dumpsters and vast grass areas for the kids to play. I also noticed garbage all over the compound consisting of garbage bags mostly outside of the apartments, furniture piled up outside the apartments and all around the dumpster areas. There were bikes – large and small- spread out all over the complex. Also, I noticed charcoal grills, some newer but most in nasty condition all around the property. In the parking lot, there were many abandoned cars with flat tires, broken car windows covered with cheap plastic blowing all over the place, and many cars that didn't have license plates.

In looking at the residential windows and patio doors, I noticed many window blinds either missing or broken. Most patio doors had missing or broken vertical blinds. Quite a few patio doors had old blankets covering them. The buildings were in decent shape. The lower part of the buildings were brick and the upper portion is steel sheet panels. I found the building design to be a bit odd. I could tell that if it rained, you would get soaked entering the homes.

The common hallways in the two-bedroom apartments were filled with garbage, bikes, shoes and strollers. At that time, I was unaware of HUD rules and regulations concerning common areas. Remember, this was the first time I was exposed to subsidized housing and the extraordinary amount of rules. Boy, was I in for a shocking, eye opening experience. So much so, the experience compelled me to keep copious notes so that someday I would write a book about it all to subsequently offer solutions.

The location of the housing complex was very close to two schools. It was located next to a school that had kindergarten through fifth grade and the other school offering sixth grade through ninth grade. I thought the location was perfect for family housing.

In looking through the tool shed and the small garage, I noticed that they were in complete disarray also. There were supplies, old and new parts, and miscellaneous tools all over the floor. Now, I was not complaining, just observing for two reasons: I loved a challenge and I had signed up to use my skills wherever they would take me. I was ready to hit the ground running!

While acclimating myself to this new challenge, I received my first maintenance call. Karen called me on my cell phone and asked me to go to building three on a maintenance request concerning an oven repair. I knocked on the door and yelled 'maintenance' and heard a voice respond 'come in.' I entered and didn't see anyone. I then responded 'hello?' At that moment, I heard moaning coming from a bedroom. I didn't know what to think. Again, this was my first day and I wasn't really sure what to do next.

I said 'hello' again as I slowly walked in. Then I heard a woman's voice asking e to come into the back bedroom. I proceeded to the room and discovered an overweight woman laying on the bed. I again said 'hello' and introduced myself as the new maintenance man. She responded 'Oh, ok. Could you please help me up so I can get my walker and show you the problem with my stove?' I was now experiencing a dilemma. I was pondering (in my mind) if it was acceptable within the confines of my duties to assist? Was I required to physically help a tenant out of a bed? What would be the consequences of aiding if there was an injury? At that moment, I did not know what to do. I decided to use my own judgment and helped her sit up very slowly.

Here was the shocker...While grabbing her very large arm and helping her sit up, I discovered she was NAKED! I thought, 'oh my God! I was not trained or prepared for this and there was no turning back.'

After a huge effort, the lady put on her robe and reached the stove to describe the oven issues. I felt she could have just told me what the problem was with the stove so I could fix it.

After repairing the stove, I proceeded to the office to inquire if what I just experienced was within the requirements of my duties. I explained the experience to Karen, the property manager and Susan -- Karen's assistant. While explaining the part of me pulling this tenant up from the bed, and that she was naked, and my eyes were as wide as saucers and I wasn't sure to keep helping her or just drop her and run out, the two just burst out laughing hysterically. I was actually relieved they were laughing. I then realized that the work atmosphere in the office was not going to be uptight nor run strictly 'by the book.'

DAY TWO

I was excited and up for the impending challenge of learning all about subsidized housing and implementing a plan to clean up the compound and add another successful project to my resume. I entered the office and Karen had lots of surprises for me. The first surprise was to watch some videos on HUD rules and regulations concerning every maintenance situation. Then I was tested on my knowledge of the material on a computer. I also had to watch REAC videos and was subsequently test on them. Note: I had no idea what REAC meant. I would find out later that REAC stood for Real Estate Assessment Center. It was a government run organization that inspected all subsidized housing projects. The inspections were grueling and had (ridiculous) standards concerning the condition of the properties. Furthermore, they ignored the fact that some tenants maintained clean and organized apartments. Later in the book I will dedicate an entire chapter on this organization.

Truthfully, I didn't really understand what I was watching, however, I did pay attention to the videos and took all of the required tests. Some of the information seemed insignificant to me (being that I was already landlord).

However, I would soon learn the scale of government involvement with regards to subsidized housing.

After I completed most of my testing for the initial onslaught of regulations that I needed to comply with, Karen brought me a three-inch binder which contained the rules and regulations we needed to practice. This was the HUD book and Karen asked me to take it home and study it. I did take it home and briefly paged through it. I concluded that the government's overreach in regulations with regards to operating a subsidized housing project was not only confusing, but overly complicated, convoluted and excessively verbose.

Upon learning about my new responsibilities, I must admit I shook my head and thought 'what the hell did I get myself into?' But once again, I was up for the challenge and felt the job would be excellent experience for me. So after the second day of being employed by a private owner of this subsidized housing project, I decided to take copious notes of the daily operations and inner personal relations with the tenants, management, HUD and REAC inspectors.

CHAPTER 2

Day three: Time to interact with the tenants

After going through all of the training videos and materials, I really wanted to start organizing a "plan of attack" to set myself up for success. I first went into the tool shed to survey what tools, equipment and supplies I had to work with -- a strategy I always used throughout my career. I quickly discovered I had limited amounts of everything I needed so I thought this would be my first challenge.

The previous maintenance person had left a disaster. I couldn't even see the floor-- there was so much junk. The tool shed measured about fifteen by fifteen feet and there was so much junk all over the place that I had to pull things out to even step foot into the shed. So that actually was my first challenge in the field. I took some pictures and started making two piles --- items to KEEP and items for the DUMPSTER.

After working on the shed for about three hours, I received a maintenance request. It was at that moment I wondered how the requests were obtained and executed.

This is what I discovered..... usually the tenants would call the office and leave a message for requests. The office staff, however, did not ever want to answer the phones (I soon found out). They would rather listen to their messages, put the requests on a priority list, and then act on them appropriately. We did have an emergency line that tenants were able to use in case the matter was something that needed immediate attention.

My first request on day three was a tenant that needed her kitchen light replaced. Now I was questioning why we were replacing light bulbs? So I knocked on the door and nobody answered. I could hear children and the television blaring. I knocked again and still nothing. I proceeded to the office to check if the tenant left a phone number. I asked the secretary and she explained to me that most of the tenants don't leave their numbers and that most didn't even have phones. I asked how the tenants called in requests and the secretary informed me they usually find someone around the complex that has a phone and they borrow it to place requests. I then explained to the secretary that I knocked on the door and heard children's' voices and a television that was on. She recommended that I **POUND** on the door and yell 'maintenance!' She said then only will they answer the door. It took me awhile to figure out why.

I discovered many tenants were afraid to open the door unless they knew who was there. Their fear and reasons encompassed several issues/circumstances of which some included:

1. They were afraid of their 'baby daddies' and they didn't want around.
2. They were afraid of bill collectors, professional servers, and social workers.
3. They were afraid of drug dealers looking for their baby daddies, boyfriends, and ex boyfriends.
4. They were afraid of the police searching for the company they kept and let stay with them.
5. They were afraid of police searching for drugs.
6. They were afraid of the humane society investigating animal abuse.
7. They were afraid of confrontation from other tenants.

These were just some of the reasons they were hesitant to open the door. In reading through these chapters, my hope was to explain in detail all of these issues.

Now getting back to my first maintenance request in building six. I returned and pounded very hard this time on the door and shouted 'MAINTENANCE!' The door opened! Before me was a very disheveled woman in her late twenties. She invited me in and showed me where the light was not working I discovered that in the kitchens of these three bedroom townhouses had two sets of lighting. There were two four -foot florescent bulbs on the ceiling and one eighteen-inch florescent light bulb above the kitchen sink. Now it made sense to me why they were calling us for lighting. Most of the tenants didn't know *how* to change those kinds of bulbs and most probably couldn't afford to change them anyways.

This was my first time in a three-bedroom townhouse. I immediately noticed that the foyer, dining room, kitchen, and downstairs bathroom right off of the dining room had vinyl floors. The living rooms have glass patio doors had carpeting. All of the walls were painted the same eggshell color. I was glad to see that because I knew it was much easier to paint an apartment the same color. The eggshell color was chosen and designated by our company and it was a universal color throughout all of the complexes.

I asked the tenant if there was anything else I could fix, and she gave me a small list. The list included water in the basement, two holes in the walls upstairs, and window blinds that needed replacing. I asked her about all of the vertical patio blinds that were destroyed or missing and she replied "don't worry about them. I like keeping my blankets over the window and door." (I replied that it was ok, it was her house. Later, in my experiences with this job, I would discover that was the wrong thing to say and I'll explain later).

Shortly thereafter, I heard dogs yelping in the basement. I asked her if she had dogs. She said she was dog sitting for a friend. I said ok. Later, I would find out that was a lie. Per policy, I later discovered dogs were not allowed on the complex unless specifically designated "service dogs." Dogs in the basements would become a bigger issue in the coming days.

And that was my very first experience in executing a maintenance request in family housing.

I returned to the office to continue to work on the tool shed when Karen informed me that we had ten empty apartments and that the company wanted them cleaned, painted, and rent ready as soon as possible. This request posed a huge challenge for me given the fact that I was the only one doing maintenance for 82 apartments at that time -- I would inherit a regional position later. I knew I had to orchestrate a comprehensive plan to achieve this tall order.

I went to investigate all of the "empties" (as we fondly called them) to check the condition of the units. I was shocked! I couldn't believe what I saw.

Virtually every apartment was trashed and unkempt! Every stove was filthy and not cared for ---caked with grease inside and out. Every refrigerator was also nasty -- new and old food left inside and in the freezer. There were bars and drawers missing from inside the refrigerator as well. Caked on food and liquid spills inside and out. It appeared these spills and stains were very old and NEVER cleaned or addressed. The kitchen floors were greasy, grimy, dirty. Spills of every imaginable grimy substance one could think of. The counter tops were all left with the same filth. Given that information, one could only guess what it looked like under the sink and in the cupboards.

Most of the apartments had lots of leftover food. Mostly canned food, old moldy bread, boxes upon boxes of products like mac & cheese, rice, gravies, etc. There were also gallons of old smelly cooking oil in cabinets and under the sinks. Everything in the kitchen of almost all of the apartments was greasy and just plain dirty.

I also noticed stains on the ceilings. Some of the stains I could not identify. Most of the stains seemed to be someone shaking up soda cans and spraying them all over the ceilings. That was my guess. In reviewing the ceilings, I also noticed missing smoke detectors, holes the size of tennis balls, and ceiling fans encrusted with at least half inch of grease, grime, and dirt. The ceiling fans had a series of three lights on them and in most apartments, only one bulb worked – if any.

I moved to the living rooms. Immediately, I noticed many holes in the walls. Not all of the ten apartments we inspected, but I would say at least half of them. The holes varied in size, but mostly the size of a fist. I also noticed that most of the patio door vertical blinds were yellow, cracked, missing, or hanging on by a thread. Not one apartment was cleaned! The carpets were filthy and gross. I later learned that our professional carpet cleaning company usually passed on most of our carpet cleaning requests. They didn't even want our business. The gentleman from the cleaning company commented that not even HE could save those carpets. Note: the bedrooms were not quite as bad and half of the time he could get them clean enough. A lot of the carpets also had long snag runs and tears.

I then moved to the downstairs half bath. Most of them were extremely dirty and smelly. Every toilet was yellow with stains. The toilet bowls were black and gray. The toilet seats were all loose and gross. There were ceiling tiles on the ceiling so that if there was a leak from upstairs -- pulling them down gave access to repair any loose or rusted out pipes. Most of the tiles were filled with stains. I found out later that the pipes never leaked. Rather, the tenants/kids overflowed the toilet and/or bathtub regularly in the upstairs bathroom located right above the downstairs half bath.

I continued to the basements -- Yes, full basements with standard washer/dryer hookups. Most of the basements were dry. However, most of the tenants left piles and piles of dirty clothes. They also left couches, old tube TV's, bikes, washers or dryers or both that usually didn't work, lots of children's toys, beds, dressers. I could go on and on. It was hard to believe what I was seeing and learning about subsidized housing.

I proceeded to the upstairs level. Most of the bathrooms were grungy, dirty, smelly. The bathtubs and toilets in most were extremely dirty. Most of the bathtubs needed the caulking replaced. I also noticed water stains and mold on the ceilings. Later in talking with the tenants, I discovered that most of the tenants and their wanted/unwanted guests take long hot showers. When I thought about it, they're not required to pay for water or to heat the water. I was beginning to see all of the abuses happening within subsidized housing.

In reviewing these empty apartments, I came across these folding closet doors. They weren't the best quality. The doors were very tall heavy steel doors that were on tracks and you had to pull for them to open. I would estimate that forty percent were bent, barely hanging, off the tracks and some were plain missing. The windows were newer vinyl and in good shape. The window blinds were metal, and most were bent or missing. There were many windows without blinds and were covered with blankets or towels. Also, I noticed many windows had old tape around them and/or were filled with kid's stickers.

The ceilings and the walls on quite a few units also had kid's stickers, crayon markings, magic marker swirls, holes and stains that were unidentifiable. Some of the carpets had many stains of red dye colored drink mixes, fingernail polish, and other stains I could not identify.

I returned to the office and sat at my desk and was confused at what I had just seen. I was comparing what I had seen to my own renters and how my tenants lived compared to what I had just witnessed. I really did not know where to start. Every apartment needed an immense amount of work to get it rent ready.

Karen came into my office to let me know that HUD didn't accept empty apartments when there was a waiting list. That meant we had to work our asses off to get these units rent ready quickly.

CHAPTER 3

Why are they moving here?

At the time I was working, there were about twenty families on our waiting list. Out of the twenty or so, only four to five families may have been accepted. I learned that if an applicant had a felony, drug or money eviction or even a disorderly conduct charge, they would not be approved for a move in. Most of the applicants were mothers from Milwaukee and Chicago looking to get out of those cities due to the violence and danger surrounding their neighborhoods.

I was surprised to see the desperation in their eyes when they came into the office to pick up an application. I tried to put them at ease with a positive attitude while maintaining a professional and calm demeanor. I explained to them to take their time filling out the 21-page application and to write legibly and to make sure all of the social security numbers were correct. I remembered most of the new applicants were very nice and appreciative. Almost all of the applicants that came in were chasing after their kids all over the office. Kids will be kids and I guessed during those interactions the mothers didn't have anybody to watch the children – which made it even more difficult for them to concentrate on the 21-page application. The kids running amuck around the office made for a stressful environment for the office staff.

In talking with these tenants, while they were applying for an apartment or townhouse, I discovered that approximately 80% of them were single African American mothers with several 'baby daddies.' Most of these mothers told me they wanted to distance themselves and their children from their deadbeat baby daddies -- there description, not mine -- and their unsafe neighborhoods. However, after they were accepted for tenancy, I found out that this was not necessarily true.

My first 'move in' was very interesting. That's when I started to understand the dynamics of different cultures and attitudes in the rental business.

It was a cold December morning when I was informed by Karen, the property manager, that we were having a move-in around 10am. This was my first experience with a move in tenant and I had to learn the process.

The first thing I needed to do was go to the pending apartment and do a quick inspection to ensure that the townhouse was ready. The requirements encompassed: a set of keys, clean or new carpeting, spotless walls, ceilings, appliances, floors, toilets, mirrors, ceiling fans, windows, window blinds, patio blinds, bathtub, faucet fixtures and much more. The tenant was given a 'move in sheet' that addressed all of these issues and we required the new tenant to complete that checklist. If there were any issues they felt were unacceptable, they were to check the appropriate 'unacceptable' area and we had to correct the problem. **Please keep in mind that most of these tenants had zero income and were given a rent-free reconditioned townhouse that included heat, water, and subsidized power and light. ** Most of these tenants also received food stamps. One would think these tenants would be extremely happy and grateful to receive these amenities without scrutiny and objections. However, this was not always the case.

My first move in arrived sixty minutes late. I greeted them and welcomed them to their new home. They just kind of stared at me and shook their heads. It was their way of saying hello – that's how I took it. The paperwork required for them to actually receive their keys usually took one hour. After the lease was signed and the property manager explained all of the rules and regulations set forth by HUD and the private owner, I was tasked with the physical walk through of the townhouse with them.

The tour was taken by the new tenant and her four children, the tenant's mother and one of the tenant's baby daddies. The baby daddy and the mother of the tenant were not on the lease but insisted on the tour.

I showed all seven individuals around the complex – explaining the rules about the playground for the kids, the grill and picnic areas, where the nearest schools were, and the dumpster area locations. We then went to the townhouse where their new home was.

I opened the front door and said with enthusiasm, "here is your new home!" They looked at me without much emotion. The children scattered through the place like fire ants on a mission. During the tour, I explained where everything was and asked them to let me know if everything looked acceptable. I noticed the new tenant was fine with everything and surprised at the overall cleanliness of the place. She noticed the freshly painted walls, clean carpets and floors, new blinds, etc. However, the grandmother (her mother) started to pick the place apart.

The grandmother didn't seem grateful for her daughter's newly renovated home nor the fact that it was situated in a very safe neighborhood. She questioned the color of the carpet and didn't like the kitchen cabinets for starters. I was floored and couldn't believe what I was hearing. We had worked very hard to renovate this subsidized townhouse that her daughter and grandchildren were receiving free. I suspected this townhouse was a total upgrade from where they were living before they moved here. I decided at that moment that I would ignore any observation or complaint from anybody that was not on the lease. Her opinion didn't matter to me or our mission of providing clean, safe, subsidized housing to our leased tenants.

Continuing the tour while ignoring the grandmother, I noticed that the baby daddy didn't say much or made much eye contact with me. I felt this was a little strange but continued with the tour. The grandmother kept telling the daughter to write down the little imperfections she noticed during the tour on the move in sheet. I had to explain as we were inspecting the townhouse that little things like scratches in the vinyl, a blemish on the carpet or even a toilet seat that wasn't brand new but clean were normal and that we didn't charge the tenant when they vacated the premises.

After the inspection was complete, I handed the mother her keys and again welcomed her and the children to their new home and assured her that we were here to help. She said 'thanks a lot' and continued to inspect.

Before I left her to get settled in, I asked when her furniture was arriving. I had noticed they all arrived in a small, beat up car. She replied "oh, I don't have any furniture.' I was a little confused. I said 'ok' and returned to the office to report to Karen how everything went.

I explained to Karen that the mother didn't say too much, and the baby daddy didn't say anything, but the grandmother picked the place apart. Karen replied, "shut the door and pull up a chair."

She then tried to explain to me the differences between government housing and private ownership rental properties.

She began by explaining that there was a certain attitude within the tenants' expectations of how they demanded to be treated and respected regardless of their situation or circumstance and/or if they paid rent or even if everything was free. She said I would soon discover that many of the tenants were _not_ appreciative of their new homes and benefits and in her own words would "wear you down on their demands, so be prepared." Hearing those words were not comforting to me – especially coming from someone who had been in government housing for a few years already.

During our conversation, the phone rang. The part time assistant answered and relayed a message to me that something was wrong in the apartment of our new move ins. I looked at Karen and she had a big smile on her face. She said, 'here we go.'

This experience was my first encounter with the "demands" Karen mentioned. Apparently, the new tenants wanted to see if we could paint the entire apartment a different color. I asked Karen if we accommodated requests like that. She replied "absolutely not." Karen explained that we were required by our company's rules that all townhouses and apartments were to be uniform in the paint color. That means all walls, ceilings, hallways, basements, etc were to painted an eggshell color bought from the same paint company with the same formula. Under no circumstances were any tenants to paint different colors in their apartments or townhouses.

Those new tenants didn't like the eggshell color and wanted it changed. They were insistent. I had to explain to them that it was company policy that everything had to be uniform. They were very unhappy with the explanation and felt it was a restriction and threatened to call HUD to file a complaint. I informed them that HUD didn't set the policy and that it would be fruitless to even try. They were very upset and rolled their eyes. Even the grandmother was disdainful – even though, again, she was not a tenant or on the lease.

The following day we had our next move-in. The tenant was a single mother with one small child that seemed timid and scared. She was receiving one of the two bedroom apartments. These apartments were located in a building with shared hallways with a basement that had storage units and laundry.

I gave her the tour of the apartment, hallways, and basement. She didn't say too much but seemed appreciative.

I introduced her to a female tenant across the hall with the hope that she'd make a contact and maybe a friend in her building so that she'd feel safer and more secure. They met and seemed friendly towards one another. After the impromptu meeting and small conversation, the neighbor retreated into her own apartment.

We then went into her new apartment to finish the move-in sheet. I then handed her keys for the basement and her front door. I asked her if she had any furniture and she replied 'no.' I asked her where she was moving from and she replied 'Chicago.' She then told me that what I saw was what she had to her name. I felt extremely sorry for her situation. I told her that we just had a move-out and that some furniture had been left behind and that the cleaning lady and I could throw some items on the Gator, a field vehicle, and bring it over to her if she wanted it. We brought her a couch, one bed, end table, and one lamp. We also gave her a sheet with the organizations that could help her obtain food and supplies. She was very appreciative and thanked us.

I asked her why she moved to Fond du Lac. She told me that she wanted to get out of Chicago due to the violence and murders in her neighborhood. She said she had a child to protect and Fond du Lac was the only city that had openings for housing. Also, she said that the baby daddy was abusive and called him an "outlaw." She also conveyed to me that she was afraid that he might find her.

Note: Try to imagine moving to another state with nothing but the clothes on your back with a small child -- No food, no furniture, no friends. That was what she was confronting and dealing with. How daunting.

At that moment, I realized that I was embarking on a whole new subculture that would require patience, empathy, and understanding. I had a lot to learn about the dynamics of government housing. I decided to keep an open mind and perform my job to the best of my ability with kindness and a willingness to understand each tenant and his/her respective situations.

CHAPTER 4

First year Police Calls

I was shocked at the exorbitant amount of police interactions with our tenants and their so-called guests. The police were called to the complex almost every day. I have chronicled most of the egregious incidents I had experienced in the six years I was employed with this company. Here is a sample of police calls my very first year.

I was working in an apartment on a toilet issue when I received a call from Karen to immediately come to the office. I dropped everything I was doing and headed to the office. When I arrived, Karen said I needed to go to building one #10 and look at the front door which needed to be repaired. I asked what happened. She said the police drug unit broke the door in and threw in a flash bomb in an attempt to arrest a drug dealer that was residing there.

So I immediately went to investigate and sure enough, the steel door was damaged and the apartment smelled as if it was the 4th of July. It smelled like fireworks in the apartment. There were about six adults sitting around, some on the floor, not saying a word. The police had already left. I asked what was going on and nobody would respond. A neighbor that witnessed the entire event told me that the police were looking for somebody named "D-man" and he wasn't there. The neighbor was laughing while explaining what happened to me.

I returned to the office and reported to Karen what had happened. I asked her when the police were coming back to fix the door. She started laughing. I was confused. I asked her why she was laughing. She replied, "hey rookie, when the MEG unit breaks a door down searching for someone, we are responsible for the repairs." I asked why? She claimed it was our responsibility to keep the criminals off the property. (Note: I soon discovered **MEG** stood for "Metropolitan Enforcement Group" which was a collection of investigators from local law enforcement agencies from different adjacent counties specifically dedicated to helping maintain a **drug free** environment in which citizens could thrive). I asked why didn't they just come to the office and ask me to let them in or get the key? She replied, "That's not how it works." So I returned to repair the steel door and it wasn't easy. While I was trying to bend the door back into shape good enough for it to be able to close, I realized the handle needed to be replaced. The so-called guests stared at me with unnerving silence. After I repaired the door, I shouted out "all done" hoping I would get a response. No response.

I came into work one morning and Karen asked me to call our glass company to order a new glass patio door. I replied "ok, why?" She said that the police were there last night and in building #3 the tenant's baby daddy (who didn't live there) tried to get into the apartment. She continued to explain that the tenant was afraid for her own safety as well as the safety of her two children, and would not unlock the front door. So he threw a huge rock through the patio glass door.

I went to the apartment to talk with the tenant and assess the damage. She told me that to her surprise, her ex-boyfriend (the baby daddy) wanted in. She told him to go away and that she wasn't going to open the door. She said he became enraged and tried to kick in the steel door but it wasn't budging. She said he then ran outside and started kicking in the patio door and throwing a huge rock at it until it broke. I asked her if she called the police. She said someone else must have (called the police) because she didn't have a phone.

I returned to the office and made arrangements for the patio glass door to be replaced. I asked Karen who pays for that? I wanted to know. She said she was going to try to have the tenant pay for the replacement door. She also added that the baby daddy wasn't arrested because he took off and was nowhere to be found. I was curious as to how the tenant would pay for the replacement glass. So I asked Karen what the protocol was if the tenant didn't pay. She replied, "Oh well, it goes down as our loss."

During that year, we received some very disturbing news from the police one morning. They came to the office to let us know that they were called to the property to investigate a case of animal cruelty. Evidently, several tenants had witnessed an incident and had called the police.

The police said a tenant in building #5 called them to report the dismembering of a cat by a five-year-old boy wearing a super hero costume. Apparently this young boy decided that he was a superhero and that his mission was to rid his house of the annoying cat. In the police report, the boy told the officers that he first beat it to death -- because he didn't want the cat to come back to life. Then he decided to tear it apart and throw the pieces around the complex. They took the boy into custody to have an evaluation of his mental state. He was subsequently put back in his mother's care that same day.

I was in building #2 fixing a tenant's stove one day and the tenant, who was an elderly lady, told me that she called the police a couple of days ago about her adjacent neighbor. She said she had called the police several times due to his blaring music. I asked if she had spoken directly with the neighbor before resorting to calling the police. She said she had spoken to the neighbor but had no cooperation. I replied that when she did that, then they know that she was the one complaining. She said 'Yeah. I know that now.' Then she said 'You wouldn't believe what he did -- I said I couldn't wait to hear her story.

She began telling me that the guy in the townhouse next to hers was outside in front of her patio window. He started what appeared to be a campfire and was performing some strange ritual and staring into her patio window and was dancing around and pointing at her. Her belief was that this was retaliation for calling the police on his extremely loud music. I told her I'd have a chat with him and would relay to him that any aggression toward another tenant was unacceptable. I asked her to let me know if he did anything like that again.

So I went over to this townhouse, explained to him that we don't allow rituals like that and that he needed to keep his music down. He didn't seem to understand due to his poor English so I had to use my hands and "make up sign language" to get my point across. He kept nodding 'yes' and saying 'ok.' He then offered me some boiled chicken feet which I respectfully declined. I had hoped he understood everything. (Sometimes the tenants weren't completely honest with how much English they really knew and understood).

One morning I was doing paperwork when the police came in to inform us that they arrested the gentleman in building four #6 for possession of narcotics. I said that I was disappointed because that tenant was a nice person. He was living with his parents; however, his father had just passed away, and his mother was in the hospital very sick.

The police said that he was going to jail for awhile due to other arrests and that he was 'on paper.' I found out 'on paper' meant that he was on probation. A sidebar to this incident is that he left his apartment a complete disaster. I had permission to enter to remove the food left out so it wouldn't mold and smell. I checked the apartment over and locked the door. However, I soon realized why it was better to have someone in an apartment than not.

We were experiencing a cold snap that winter when the circulating pump for the water heat stopped working. (The pump circulated hot water through the floor registers and kept the entire building warm). Unfortunately, we hadn't noticed when exactly the pump went out. So the building started to cool down. When I noticed that the pump wasn't working, I immediately called to have it replaced; however, the repair took 6 hours.

During that time, the temperature in the building dropped dramatically while outside temperatures plummeted below zero with severe wind chills. The pump was replaced and we were successful in getting in running. A couple days later, however, the building was getting cold again. I thought the boiler went out so I went to investigate. I discovered the boilers were working and same with the new pump. Good news. A little perplexed, I peeked into the crawl space for any other clues. I found water flowing down from the floors like Niagara Falls. I immediately thought "Oh my God. That's the apartment that I was just in two days prior checking things out due to the tenant going to jail."

Apparently, what happened was the floor pipes had frozen and split. So when the pump was repaired, the pipes thawed out and water filled the entire apartment. All of the tenants' belongings left on the floors were soaked and destroyed. The floors were now buckled and destroyed as well. And all of this happened due to a tenant being arrested for drugs. It was an absolute nightmare renting a POD and storing all of their salvageable household items for three months while the necessary repairs were made.

The tenant finally returned from jail and was evicted for drug use that was documented. Side note: Without a police report or conviction, even if we knew they were consuming or selling drugs, we had no recourse and could not evict anyone. I will have more about this story later in the book.

I was in the tool shed one afternoon when a tenant knocked on the door. She had some information for me about a townhouse adjacent to hers. She told me that the police had been casing the place searching for "T-man." I didn't know T-man so I asked her who that was. She said that it was an uncle of the lady that lived in that townhouse. She also mentioned that she hadn't seen anyone coming or leaving the house in awhile and asked me to check it out.

I knocked on the door. No answer. I then returned to the office to obtain an right to enter form. I filled it out and posted it on the door. By law, we are required to give tenants a 12-hour advance notice to enter their apartment or townhouse – unless it was a welfare check or building emergency.

The following day I returned to enter and inspect the place. I pounded on the door several times yelling 'maintenance.' Many times, the tenants were sleeping all times of the day and didn't hear the door knocks. Over time, I realized I had to yell 'maintenance' extremely loud or they wouldn't answer -- as I eluded too earlier. I also learned that many tenants were afraid to answer the door due to people looking for them or stalking them. This was something I mentioned before.

I entered cautiously. At first, there didn't seem to be anything strange except for the fact that all of the lights were on. I began to inspect the townhouse for anything unusual. I went upstairs to see if anyone was home. I discovered all of the clothes in the closets were gone -- so were the dressers. Everything in the bathroom was also gone. I went back downstairs and saw the television was gone. I then thought to myself "midnight movers."

Midnight movers --as we called them, were tenants who grabbed their clothes, televisions (if they had one), toiletries and proceeded to skip out of town – usually at night. They usually left everything else for us to dispose of. Typically, everything left behind was so beat up we had to either dispose of it or give salvageable items to other tenants – including unopened food. (We found out later from the police that they were watching this townhouse due to reports that the tenant and her guests had a meth lab in the basement).

Earlier in this book I was describing my first maintenance request and discovered that the tenant had dogs in the basement. I mentioned that the dogs would become a huge issue later – and they did. That anecdote yet to come.

There were many times we had to call police. One incident occurred one afternoon when I was doing routine maintenance calls. I was driving my utility vehicle going from apartment to apartment when I discovered a gathering of African American men and Asian men in an open patch of grass on the side of our office building. They started to square off and form a line between them. The incident reminded me of the musical West Side Story.

They were all yelling obscenities across enemy lines. I began to chuckle. The Asians were speaking in their foreign language and the African Americans were yelling in their cultural slang. Neither group seemed to be able to understand one another. However, they were brandishing weapons. The African Americans had baseball bats and sticks and the Asians had butter knives -- it was a stand off!

I went into the office laughing and reported to Karen about the stand-off and mentioned we might want to call the police. We were watching out of our window when the police finally arrived. When the police went to break up the standoff, the Sharks and Jets saw the police coming and they all scattered.

Such incidents were just a small example of the police calls we experienced on almost a daily basis. More of these examples throughout this book would ensue.

CHAPTER 5

24 Senior Citizen Units

Our company owned approximately many complexes around the United States. Our division had the distinct task of running and maintaining four of these properties while offering support to many others.

One of our responsibilities was to operate a 36-senior citizen unit complex in a town about 50 miles away. These units were one-bedroom apartments that shared common hallways and laundry rooms. The complex offered plenty of off-street parking and was surrounded by grass, trees, and pretty bushes. Heat, water, and storage units were all included in their rent and the tenants were responsible for their own electric bills.

Some of the tenants paid 30% of their income for rent while others paid zero rent due to zero income. Those tenants without income were called "zero renters." These zero renters also received vouchers from the power and light companies. They also qualified for food stamps. Whatever their situation, we treated each and every one of them with the respect they deserved.

My first time at the senior citizen units, I was tasked to go and perform my first maintenance call. I was given the keys and location and was basically on my own. I always enjoyed those types of challenges.

I found the location and gave myself a quick tour through the 3 buildings. I discovered that the basements, hallways, storage units, parking lot and overall grounds were extremely clean and organized. I noticed there was an extremely different atmosphere and attitude surrounding this property and it seemed that almost everyone that lived in these buildings had respect for the property. I was pleasantly surprised and couldn't wait to get started.

My first request was to repair a garbage disposal that was plugged. I arrived at the apartment and introduced myself to the tenant. He seemed nice, however, he also seemed young to be a tenant there given the fact that it was a 55 and older complex. Nonetheless, I reviewed the issue with the garbage disposer and why it was plugged.

This is what happened. The tenant decided to clean the fish he had caught the past couple of days in the bathtub and kitchen sink. This process plugged both drains. I asked him if he knew that this was a bad decision. He replied "well, I just figured the disposer would take care of the fish scales – no problem." I shook my head and replied "ok, I'm going to fix both drains but if this happens again I am going to have to charge you." He replied "really?" I responded "really!" He wasn't too happy. A few months later I decided to remove the garbage disposer to eliminate future calls.

In working there, I found quite the dichotomy of the generation gap between family housing and senior housing.

It seemed however, the generation at the senior complex had a different way of conducting themselves. They seemed to keep their apartments cleaner and more organized. They also seemed to respect the condition of everything associated with their building and surroundings. The tenants were very thankful when I took care of their requests. My experience at the senior housing was opposite to what I was used to at the family housing complexes.

We had a tenant that had chronic back problems that was receiving social security for her ailment. She was in her 40's and was living in an upstairs apartment. When I met her, she seemed very nice but a little edgy. We received an anonymous call at our office that she had someone living with her. This was not allowed. For someone to live in the complex, they had to apply and be approved by the corporate office and then be added to the lease. It was quite the process. This lady had not done that and he was there illegally.

Additionally, we had reports that he was breaking into cars -- and also breaking into apartments. We couldn't catch him nor could we kick him off of the property. It was extremely difficult to prove that someone was living with a tenant illegally. We basically had to take pictures of their mail and the address to begin the eviction process against the tenant. When we submitted to them a warning of eviction, the perpetrator usually vacated the premises only to return later. These were not rules set by the company. Instead, these were government (HUD – Housing and Urban Development) rules.

Eventually I had words with him directly. He was working on his car in the parking lot when I approached him to confront him of the situation. I was upfront with him about the rumors that were circulating around the complex. I told him that there were reports that he was living there and that he was breaking into cars and apartments searching for drugs. Remember, this was senior living and many of the residents had medicines for ailments related to aging. He denied all allegations and maintained he wasn't living there. I responded, "Dude. You're lying -- we all know you're living here and if you don't move, your girlfriend will be forced to forfeit her apartment." He replied, "whatever."

Eventually his girlfriend called the police on him and claimed he stole her medication and he moved. That particular situation prompted us to install deadbolts to all entry doors to the apartments. The cost to the complex was enourmous.

A couple of weeks later, we moved this tenant to a lower unit due to her disability. She was having a hard time with the steps going up to her apartment. Personally, I hated transfers. First, we had to refurbish the apartment they were transferring *from*. Then we had to refurbish the apartment they were transferring *to*. And remember, their security deposit was usually $30.00. With such a low deposit, why would anyone take the time and effort to clean! So the reality was that we were refurbishing two apartments for one tenant at our cost. One might ask why we didn't charge the tenants for repairs and cleaning? The simple answer was that in most cases, the tenants didn't have any income and we were not allowed to charge them. All of this was common knowledge with the tenants. More specifics on this topic later in the book.

This tenant transferred to another building into a fully refurbished apartment. She immediately complained about the brand new carpet claiming she didn't like brown carpet. I asked her why. I mentioned the color hid stains, wear marks, and looked newer far longer than cream color. She replied that with brown carpeting, she would have to vacuum more often. I thought to myself in that instant, "Really? You sit around here all day with nothing to do -- how lazy can one person be?" I kept that thought to myself.

She moved in and it wasn't even one week she had a different guy living with her. We found out that everyone called him Jerimiah.

It was less than a week when the tenants in this building started to catch me in the halls to place complaints. They all basically said they smelled weed in the hallway almost every time they left and returned from the building. They complained it was so pungent that it made some of them nauseous.

I approached this tenant to let her know about the complaints. I asked her who this person was and why he was living with her – which was a lease violation. She told me that he was her daughter's husband and that he was homeless and that he only stayed over just occasionally. She assured me that he was not smoking marijuana and that he was leaving soon.

A couple of weeks later, a tenant informed us that there was a warrant for his arrest and that he was still living there. Tenants in these buildings have a way of finding out information about rule breakers! We called the police to inform them that a fugitive was hiding out in one of our apartments. We supplied the police with his name and apartment he was staying in. They made several attempts to arrest him. Unfortunately, this tenant wouldn't open the door when the police were there. The police subsequently obtained a search warrant.

We obtained the police report after they finally arrested him with the search warrant. It was reported the police arrived around 10am and knocked on the door. Nobody answered. They heard voices and continued to pound on the door yelling "we have a search warrant. Open the door or we will force our way in!" Finally, she opened the door. They conducted their search and found the subject under the bed. He reluctantly came out from under the bed and they handcuffed him. They proceeded to take him out to the squad car when he appeared to pass out. They put him in the back seat and had an officer monitor him. Jerimiah appeared to be passed out; however the officer that was monitoring him said that he caught Jerimiah peeking out at him. Obviously, he was faking that he was passed out. They officers told Jerimiah that they were on to him and that it would be in his best interest to cooperate. The report also stated that Jerimiah was screaming all the way to the police station "black lives matter."

When I read the report I had to chuckle. I thought this was a funny incident. So I decided to talk to this tenant about the whole situation. I explained to her that harboring a fugitive was an automatic eviction and that it was a HUD requirement. She seemed surprised and defended her actions and threatened to sue everyone involved.

She complained that the only reason she was turned in was because Jerimiah was a black man. I immediately replied with much disdain to her comment and told her I was offended. I explained to her that his skin color had nothing to do with it. I also let her know that not one person mentioned the color of his skin and that we had all types of ethnicity as tenants and that no issues had occurred like this incident.

I told her tenants hide guests all of the time and nobody complained unless there was an issue. I explained to her the big issue was the pungent smell of marijuana in the hallways and that I had warned her. She wasn't buying my explanation and said, "I will see your company in court." (Note: She did retain a state paid lawyer, paid by the taxpayers of this state, who did represent her. She subsequently lost her case and was evicted. She refused to move, and we ended up paying the sheriff's office to have her physically removed.

I had a maintenance call there one day for a bathtub that was draining slowly. Upon my arrival, this tenant had a visitor and they were sitting in the living room smoking cigarettes. The company policy is no smoking in any building or on the grounds with the exception of the designated smoking shelter we had built outside.

I was snaking the bathtub drain when she approached me and asked me if she could talk to me when I was done. I said no problem. I completed the task and went to see what was on her mind. She asked me if I would repaint her entire apartment. She didn't like the yellow color. I replied, "that's not gonna happen." She seemed surprised. I said, "really? You sit around here and smoke cigarettes and turn the walls yellow and you want us to repaint?" She replied, "ah yeah! I paid taxes all my life and now I want some of that back." I tried to explain to her that paying taxes was not a savings plan. Moreover, paying taxes was for our military to keep us safe, for our roads we travel on, our bridges we cross etc., and that social security was a savings plan. She wasn't impressed. She still wanted her apartment repainted.

Overall, the attitudes and level of gratitude was a stark difference at family housing. One afternoon we were conducting a HUD inspection of random apartments –(they usually inspect 75% of apartments in a 36-unit property, and we were in this tenant's apartment when he actually thanked us and HUD for allowing him to live there). I looked at the inspector and he returned the confused look and I said "Wow! Nobody has ever said that to me!" The inspector agreed. He said that in all the years he had been inspecting government properties that nobody had ever said thank you.

Here is what we usually heard. Or what was requested of us:

1. "When are they going to plow the parking lot?"
2. "When are they going to shovel my sidewalk?"
3. "When are they going to mow the grass?"
4. "Why does that tenant get two parking spots? (when there is plenty of parking anyway)
5. "Why is that tenant using my parking spot?" (when there is not designated parking)
6. "Why is his storage unit bigger than mine?"
7. "Why do I have this color carpet? Can I get new carpet with a different color?"
8. "It's too cold in the laundry room bathroom"
9. "Why can that guy work on his car in the parking lot? It looks ghetto."
10. "The dumpsters are too far away from me."
11. "I lost my keys. Can you come open my door for me and bring me a new set of keys?"
12. "Can you replace the light bulb in my kitchen?"
13. "Can you replace the drip pans on my stove?"
14. "Can you help me hang this picture?"
15. "Can I move to a downstairs apartment?"

Those were just some of the requests and complaints we dealt with on a daily basis. Some of the requests were reasonable and we felt some were not. Again, most of the tenants were basically living there for free. The ones that did pay rent were only required to pay 30% of their income. Example: If their income was $1000/month, they only had to pay $300. The $300 included everything except electricity. In addition, most of the tenants were eligible for a food card and power and light voucher.

Overall, most of the senior tenants were very nice and respectful. I enjoyed helping them with their requests and concerns. When their requests were unreasonable, I let them know.

CHAPTER 6

The 186-unit complex in the big city

I was asked by my superior to go to the big city to help the maintenance crew prepare for a REAC inspection that was scheduled in 30 days. REAC (real estate assessment center) was a subdivision of HUD.

I was asked to join a team of maintenance employees with the goal of entering every apartment and repairing anything that we could have been flagged with.

These inspections were brutal to any maintenance person or crew. Depending on the overall scores, the inspections could be anywhere from a yearly occurrence to once every four years. The preparations were so intense that we had to hire outside experts that specialized in pre-inspection work. Subsequently, these experts would submit a comprehensive list of what needed to be corrected.

These pre-inspections cost us anywhere from $5,000-$10,000 per property. The inspections usually took one to two full days – depending on the number of units per property. The experts inspected the entire grounds, apartments, office buildings, boiler rooms, etc. Their list of potential violations was quite daunting and extensive.

Some examples:

1. If there was a single screw in a light switch cover missing, that's a level 2 violation.
2. If there was a crack in a switch or outlet cover, that's a level 2 violation.
3. If there was a crack in a window, that's a level 3 violation.
4. If there was a buckle in the carpeting, that's a trip hazard and a level 2 violation.
5. If there was a hold in the wall, that's a level 1 violation.
6. If there was a hold in the wall that had been repaired but not painted, that's a level 1 violation.
7. If any faucets were dripping, that's a level 1 violation.
8. If a drain was leaking, that's a level 2 violation.
9. If the toilet was loose or the seat was loose or it flushed slowly, that's a level 2 violation.
10. If a light bulb was missing from the socket, that's a level 2 violation.
11. If the ceiling fan was inoperable or the blades were loose, that's a level 1 violation.
12. If the sinks didn't have stoppers to hold the water in, that's a level 1 violation.
13. If a kitchen drawer didn't work properly, that's a level 1 violation.
14. If the refrigerator seal was cracked, that's a level 2 violation.
15. If a bracket in the refrigerator was bent or missing, that's a level 1 violation.
16. If an inside door didn't latch when it closed it was a level 2 violation.

These were just a few of the violations that were usually recorded. These violations had to be corrected within 30 days unless it was a level 3. Level 3 violations had to be addressed immediately. Try to imagine an inspector inspecting 25% of 186 units. Now also imagine that this was family housing where the lack of respect for the apartment and the grounds was persistent in most cases. It was quite daunting for the maintenance crew and the property manager that supervised the units. In my tenure with family housing, most of the tenants (not all) knew that if they broke things, they would not be charged. More on that topic later.

The inspectors also inspected the grounds, building exteriors, common areas, utility rooms, offices, children's playground equipment, parking lots, storage rooms and sidewalks.

A few examples of findings:

1. If the sidewalk had a portion ¾ inch higher than its counterpart, it was a level 2 violation.
2. If a sidewalk had cracks wider than 3/8 inch, it was a level 1.
3. If the parking lot had a pothole, it was a level 2.
4. If there were weeds/grass growing in between cracks, it was a level 1.
5. If the building had cracks that were not filled in, it was a level 2.
6. If a building had a hold 3/8 inch wide, it was a level 2.
7. If the building had brick and parts were chipping and not repaired, it was a level 2.
8. If a common door with a closer didn't close tight, it was a level 2.
9. If an electric junction box had a knockout missing, it was a level 3.
10. If an electric junction box had a missing cover, it was a level 3.
11. If an auto shutoff outlet with its own breaker didn't work properly, it was a level 3.

As one might imagine, the inspections were brutal -- and all inspections were based upon a complicated point system. The factors that were taken into consideration involved property size and percentage of the households -- which were then tabulated to create the property's own point system.

The point system went to 100. If the score was in the 60's, it was a fail. That was catastrophic to the mission of the company. A low score in the 60's meant that the company was not allowed to buy any new properties. This company I worked for was all about expanding. It was hard for anyone to imagine the stress and pressure endured by the maintenance crew throughout this process.

It truly was "all hands on deck" after we received the notice of the inspection. The company usually requested an extension of the inspection date. The reason for that was usually that the property would never earn a passing grade. This was due to a lack of maintenance people required to fix things throughout the year and because things were being abused and destroyed by people that just didn't care. Like I have always maintained, after the first month employed in family housing "they break things faster than we can fix them." Another factor was that in most cases, the tenants would not call for repairs because their apartment was a disaster by being dirty, messy, filthy, or hiding someone there illegally.

After we received a notice for a REAC inspection, we posted every tenants' door for the apartment to be inspected. We then hired a pre-inspector to give us a comprehensive report on the violations that needed to be addressed.

In the case of our 186-unit complex, the company decided to fly in their own expert and amass a maintenance crew from around the state. They put everyone up in hotel rooms and together began to devise a plan. I happened to be one of the lucky ones chosen.

The first day was eye opening. I arrived at 7:30am after driving 70 miles from my home-based property. The office was closed and nobody was around. I wasn't happy. I was ready to hit the ground running to complete this project. I called the project supervisor with no answer. They finally started showing up at the office around 8:30am. I was thinking that there didn't seem to be any sense of urgency.

After everyone arrived, we had a maintenance meeting to coordinate a strategy to inspect and repair every single townhouse and apartment. The supervisor gave us a checklist for each apartment we were targeting. He said to only fix the most important violations first, then move on to the next apartment or townhouse. I would like to note that the reason there were so many violations in these places was twofold. One, the company only employed the least amount of employees possible. Two, the maintenance departments usually worked at a steady pace and were reactive as opposed to proactive. With this work ethic and attitude, repairs got backed up to a point of no return. It took an inspection from HUD or REAC to get things repaired. I was very surprised to experience this type of lethargic attitude.

During the meeting, the supervisor wanted us to have security guards accompany us with the inspections. He said there were some people that were dangerous and not willing to open the door. He also said that all the doors were posted with the day their townhouse or apartment would be inspected. We were obligated to give a 12-hour notice to enter their home.

I recommended that we separate into teams with at least one of the maintenance guys that the tenants were familiar with. That way they might be more willing to comply. Then we would not need a security guard. That suggestion was discussed and agreed upon.

My team was comprised of myself, Jim (a maintenance man from one of our Michigan properties), and Quincy, the head maintenance man from that property. I asked Quincy if he would take us through an empty apartment to give us an idea of the layout. This would afford us ideas on what type of supplies we needed to load the car up with as we drove from apartment buildings to townhouses.

He gave us a tour of our first two-bedroom apartment. When we entered I noticed that most of the furniture was gone. He said that the tenant, a woman and her kid were "midnight movers." That was a term we used for tenants that moved out without notice. I noticed that she left most of her kitchen dishware, utensils, gallon jars of old smelly used cooking oil, food, etc. This was not unusual. Quincy then proceeded to take us to the first bedroom saying "you gotta see this in here."

When I entered the bedroom I noticed that it was empty. I also noticed a strange red like paint all over the cream carpeting and one wall. It was like someone laid a 4 foot by 4-foot piece of plywood on the floor and sprayed red all around it, then sprayed all over the wall leading to the hallway. I said to Quincy that I had seen a lot of strange things being a landlord and maintenance guy, however, I had never seen anything like this. I asked "what the hell is this?"

Quincy said that it was a bank bomb. He said apparently the tenant had some bad dudes living with her illegally and they robbed a bank. They brought the money back to the apartment, laid it on a table that was in the room and opened the bag. To their huge surprise, one of the packs of money had a red dye bomb in it and was designed to explode when opened. We all began laughing. Quincy said "they opened the bag, it exploded in their faces temporarily blinding them. That's when they used the wall to guide themselves to the bathroom to wash the dye out of their eyes." We looked in the bathroom and the walls, sink and floor were all covered in red dye. Quincy then said angrily, "dem boys are a bunch of dumb fucks and deserved it." We laughed about that all day!

We then proceeded to load up my car with supplies needed for repairs. Our task that day was to inspect and repair things in at least 25 apartment and townhouses.

Our first inspection was townhouses. These townhouses had a basement on one level, kitchen on the next level. One bathroom and two bedrooms on the next level, and one bathroom and bedroom on the fourth level. I said whoever designed these townhouses should be forced to live in one of these for one full year. The maintenance and upkeep with this many levels was ridiculous.

We approached our first inspection and Quincy knocked on the door and said 'maintenance.' No answer. I could hear noises inside and asked Quincy to step aside. I pounded extremely hard on the door and yelled "maintenance, inspections!" We heard a man's voice say "go away." I yelled, "your door was posted and we have a key to get in, now open the door or we're gonna let ourselves in!" I found out that we had to sound unafraid and forceful to get results. A guy finally opened the door and said to make it quick. I asked him if he was on the lease and living there and he replied "nope, not me." We all knew he was lying. I let him know we were here to inspect and repair. Quincy was impressed with my technique and said "dude, you got balls!"

The first inspection was a blueprint of what to expect going forward. We found the kitchen drains leaking all over the inside cabinet and on the floor. The cabinet and floor was buckled and warped. I asked the guy that opened the door how long the drain had been leaking? He replied that he didn't know but probably 3 months. I respectfully yelled "three months! Why didn't someone call the office?" To which he replied "no clue why. It's not my problem." And I responded, "no, now it's our problem."

I continued with the inspection. I was responsible for inspecting all of the plumbing and Quincy had the windows, doors, closet doors, trip hazards, etc., and Jim was tasked for all electrical outlets, switches, lights, ceiling fans, circuit breakers, etc. I inspected the first bathroom and discovered the toilet in pieces. It was broken in half. This was a severe health and safety violation. The toilet had exposed sharp edges. In this condition, anybody could slip and fall on the sharp edges and be severely injured. Again, I had words with that same individual and asked him how long the toilet had been broken. He replied, "a long time. Maybe 4 months or so but we called a couple of times over to that office." I went to Quincy and said "Quincy! What the fuck? This is a dangerous situation!" And he replied, "we don't have enough help. They break things faster than we can fix em."

We continued through the townhouse discovering many more issues. I began to realize that there were more repair issues than we could perform. We had to meet our deadlines before the inspection. I advised my team to repair all of the level 3's, and level 2's first – and then move to the next townhouse.

We proceeded to the next townhouse. The first repair was that the front storm door was missing its windows and screens. I asked Quincy what was up with the door? He said that most of the storm doors around the complex had issues like this. I said it was unacceptable. I said either we need to repair them all, or remove them all. I figured out early in this position that it was better, inspection-wise, to remove all storm doors, closet doors, and their floor and ceiling guides than it was to continue to repair them. I ordered the entire maintenance staff to remove all doors that needed repair. We ordered extra dumpsters to complete this task.

We spent three full days repairing holes in walls, broken toilets, dripping faucets, missing smoke detectors, broken blinds, oven repairs, plugged drains, crayon and magic markers all over the walls, missing light bulbs, closet doors off their tracks, cracked windows, broken outlets and switches, moldy bathroom walls and ceilings, broken doors, holes in doors, missing door knobs and hardware, etc.

We also had a task force working on all of the outside issues. They worked on all of the landscaping including: replacing all of the bark around the buildings, trimming bushes which had to be trimmed 6 inches from every building, cracks or trip hazards on any sidewalk, all outside lights, all playground equipment, all blacktop issues, roofs, gutters, etc. We also had a task force working on all common areas that included hallways in the high rise apartments which included all entry doors, entry steps, inside lighting, holes in walls, loose railings, gross garbage chutes, etc.

After returning back to my home-based office, I was in the process of writing down some last minute notes for future inspections when the company's national exterminator account manager stopped in. We started chatting about the accounts our region was responsible for. He had mentioned our account in the big city as he called it. He said that he was in a townhouse inspecting when the tenant's "guest" told him to leave. He replied "but I am not done inspecting." The guest told him "something was going down and to get the fuck out."

The exterminator said that he grabbed his gear and when he stepped outside he heard a gunshot coming from his left followed by a gunshot followed by his right. He said he was in the crossfire of a gunfight. He said he hit the ground until the gunfight seemed to be over and got the hell out of there. He then called his corporate office and let them know what had happened and that he personally will never step foot on that property again. I knew that it was not funny, but I had to laugh. To me, it was just another day in the life of servicing government housing. All of us, including maintenance personnel, plumbers, HVAC technicians, painters, cleaning personnel, fire department inspectors, electricians, REAC inspectors, HUD inspectors, carpet and flooring installers, landscapers etc all learned to perform our jobs with eyes behind our backs. I also wanted to state that not all of the tenants were suspect to aggression or scrutiny. There were many very nice and respectful tenants that helped make our jobs worth it.

I hope this information painted a picture of the arduous task of preparing for an inspection. I agreed with the government on conducting these inspections; however, the standards were way too strict and it was extremely difficult to maintain these standards in family housing. When Quincy said that they break it faster than we can fix it, to me that was an understatement.

CHAPTER 7

Poop Adventures

I was sitting in my office conducting bookwork when our part time secretary popped in and said we had a situation in one of the apartment buildings. She said she received a call that someone had shit in the basement hall going into the laundry room. I took my cleaning lady with me to investigate.

We proceeded into the basement and the nasty smell hit us immediately. We discovered a huge pile of human shit on the floor next to the door entering the laundry room. That door had a lock on it and only the tenants had a key that gave them access to the laundry room. **Where** our little gift as I called it was left was important because whoever did this didn't have a key to enter the laundry room where it was more private.

The chemistry of this 'gift' was weird. It was a very large fluffy piece of crap that was twirled perfectly. It appeared to be a piece of art by the discerning experts of dung. We had to laugh. I decided to grab two shovels and the two of us scooped it up. While human poop scooping, we noticed it wasn't your normal texture. It appeared to have an airy look to it. Yup! And it was fluffy and stunk to high heaven.

After the messy clean up, I started knocking on doors to ask if anyone knew who did it. One tenant said she thought it was the Hmongs living across from her. I asked why she thought that. She said she sees a lot of them coming and going all hours of the night. So I asked the Hmong tenant if she knew anything about it and she said she didn't.

About a week later, it happened again! I immediately went to see the Hmong tenant whose name is Chee. I told her we had a witness that said she had seen one of her 'guests' going down the steps into the basement. Chee claimed that it wasn't any of her friends. I didn't believe her. I found out that her husband was illegally living with her and he was the one bringing all of these people over to party and sleep on floors overnight. I warned her that we would evict her if this kept happening.

One week later, Karen informed me that Chee requested a lower apartment due to her special needs child. So we refurbished a lower apartment in another building across the complex. Once again, I never liked transfers but we subsequently transferred her to a lower unit.

It wasn't one week after the transfer when we received a complaint from Chee's building that someone shit in the basement. This meant that I was right that one of her husband's "guests" had been the "elusive crapper."

I knocked on her door with vigor. She answered the door with her sad eyes and said "yes?" I asked her if her husband was home. She said yes and went to get him. I looked at him and said come with me. He followed me into the basement and I paraded him to the pile of crap. I asked him if he knew English and he replied "wittle." I used Chee as an interpreter. I told him this was happening in this building now and now that they were here, it doesnt take a rocket scientist to figure out who's doing it.. I told him that I knew now for sure that it was his friends and if it happened again, everyone was moving. He shook his head ok. That was the last time anybody left us a gift such as that.

The next poop incident came in the form of art on the walls. Karen had warned me that she was evicting a tenant due to a drug arrest by one of the tenant's guests. This tenant was harboring a couple of drug dealers in her basement. One of them was arrested for dealing drugs and the detectives found evidence in her townhouse. That meant an automatic eviction. She received her notice and decided not to fight the eviction process and midnight moved. I was worried how this tenant and her drug-dealing guests would leave the condition of the apartment.

I have learned through my new experiences in government/public housing that 95% of move outs left the apartment or townhouse a complete disaster. Please do not think I am exaggerating! I possess many photos that would blow your mind and have decided not to use them in this book out of respect to the tenants who were fleeing for their safety or the tenants that do care how they leave the place.

We received word from a tenant that they midnight moved and that the front door was left open. I took my cleaning lady with me to do an inspection. We knocked on the door and yelled "maintenance!" There was no response so we entered slowly. We noticed that most of the household things were still in there. We always went right to the bedrooms to inspect. HUD rules were that if the clothes, beds, and toiletries were gone, that indicated abandonment and we could change the locks and start removing everything that was left behind.

We discovered that the beds and clothes were gone and the townhouse was abandoned. We continued our inspection and proceeded into the living room. All of the shitty, smelly furniture was abandoned and left for us to dispose. I looked at the south living room wall and discovered a nice little message that was left for us. I asked the cleaning lady to look at the wall. I wanted her reaction to the message. She read it, looked at me and started laughing hysterically. You see, the message written in great big letters out of human poop said "fuck all of you fuckers." Now, we were used to that type of language, however the message was written in human shit. I thought 'seriously? You have a fucking free townhouse that you were illegally dealing drugs out of and you have the audacity to blame us for the eviction and trash the place, leave us all of the furniture, moldy food, basement full or old moldy clothes, toys, washer and dryers that are inoperable, old shitty bikes, etc? and then smear human shit all over the walls?' I thought I was in a third world country. I couldn't believe it but there it was!

I was called out to our senior living complex one day due to a tenant's toilet being plugged up. This was a gentleman that told me he was having a hard time taking a crap (his words not mine) and that the toilet was plugged. So I began snaking it with my electric drill and snake. I worked on it for at least 35 minutes. Nothing was working. I decided to pull the toilet, turn it upside down and snake it from the bottom up. To my amazement, there was a turd stuck in the bottom the size of a baseball and just as hard. I felt bad for the tenant and myself. I had to use an oversized screwdriver to tear the turd apart. I finally got the turd out and reinstalled the toilet. I told him that he was a "two flusher." That meant that he should flush the first turd right away and second flush everything else. This method would help him and he thanked me up and down. I said it was no problem. I enjoyed helping our seniors because they generally appreciated our help and more importantly, they say 'thank you.'

One day I was called to a tenant's townhouse to field a complaint of a weird smell coming from an adjacent basement. She took me into her basement and asked me to examine the smell coming from her south wall. I could smell the nasty odor just walking down the steps. It reminded me of the bat exhibit at the zoo. NASTY ODOR! She said she heard dogs barking all night. I determined that the adjacent tenant was harboring dogs in the basement of his townhouse. I told her that I would take care of it and get to her about our strategy to remedy the stench and barking.

I went to the office to report my findings to Karen. We decided to give the tenant in question a 24-hour notice of inspection by law. I told Karen that they were going to remove the dogs before we inspected. She said there was nothing we could do about a surprise inspection unless it was an emergency.

We posted the door for an impending inspection. The following day I knocked on the door and yelled "inspection!" Fong, the tenant answered the door and motioned for me to enter. I told him about the smell and that I needed to go into the basement. He nodded his head as if he didn't know English. I proceeded into the basement and discovered the enormous stench. There were no dogs present which told me they removed them and tried to clean the floor.

The stench was so bad, I could not stay down there very long. Apparently, they let the dogs roam around pissing and crapping all over the basement without cleaning it up until the day before inspection.

We wrote them up for a lease violation for having dogs without a medical reason. I gave Fong some cleaning agents and told him to scrub the basement floor and hose it down the drain. He did what I asked however, it didn't work. It still stunk! I ended up painting the entire floor with polyurethane paint two times to help eliminate the smell. Note: no expense to the tenant.

In a different building and townhouse we received a call from a concerned tenant that the tenant next to her had dogs in the basement that cried and barked 24/7. I thought 'here we go again.' We posted a 24-hour notice to enter. The following day I pounded on the door to no answer. I entered the townhouse slowly. I was afraid that the dogs were loose. I could hear a loud and deep bark coming from the basement. I was contemplating opening the door when a woman walked in and said "don't open that door! There's a pit bull down there and he's not friendly." I asked the lady where the tenants were.

She said that Latisha packed up and left a week ago. I responded "great!" sarcastically.

I could smell dog shit and piss throughout the townhouse. I had a bad feeling about the dogs in the basement because I could only hear one barking. So I called our local animal shelter and asked for a rescue unit. A lady from the shelter showed up a couple of hours later and asked what apartment and what kind of dog that needed to be rescued. I said a pit bull. She rolled her eyes and said 'no kidding.' She said with much disdain, "why is it that every time I have to rescue a dog at a housing project it's a hostile pit bull?" She said she was going to call for backup and that she'd come find me when the task was completed.

She retrieved the pit bull and said she had some disturbing news. She said that there was a small dog in the basement yet that had starved to death. I uttered under my breath, "those mother fuckers!" It truly bothered me to even write about this incident. I had a hard time holding back tears.

We removed the poor thing and began the cleanup. That too was another basement we had to scrub and paint with polyurethane.

CHAPTER 8

Emergency calls during off office hours

In government housing, the company that owned the property/ properties were responsible for all health and safety issues 24 hours a day. If the company didn't respond to these calls, the tenant had the option of calling HUD to also field the emergency. As a professional company and wanting to stay in good standing with the government agency that subsidized most of the rents paid by taxpayers, it was our supreme goal not to get HUD involved. In our mission statement, we took all health and safety issues very seriously.

Here was how the "after hours" emergency call worked. The tenant placed a call into the emergency line. They left a message and waited for a return call or for someone to show up to the address of concern. The call reached an emergency line and went directly to the property manager. The property manager would field the call and determine if it was a legitimate call that needed to be addressed. If determined that it was legitimate, the property manager either called the police for safety reasons or forwarded the call to the maintenance department.

The maintenance department then received a call from an automated call center where we could listen to the tenant's recording of the call. We then had to respond immediately no matter what the nature of the call was.

My personal experiences with off hour emergency calls was extremely frustrating. I received bogus, stupid, frustrating calls at all times of the night. Some of the calls were legitimate, but most of the calls could have waited until office hours the following day. Imagine just putting in a long, hard day of work, you get home, take a shower, finally sit down to eat dinner, and the emergency line starts ringing. The first thing I would do is yell out loud "now fucking what?" I had just completed a normal day of fixing shit the tenants destroyed and didn't have to pay for, cleaning up garbage all over the grounds, dealing with unreasonable tenants, etc. -- or the emergency line rang late at night while I was sleeping. It was the worst part of the job.

Also, if I had to field an emergency call and physically go to the complex to address and fix the issue, I would **not** receive emergency pay. The company would give our maintenance guys two hours off with pay for that trip to the property. If you asked any maintenance person, they would much rather be paid to be on call. The company saved lots of money executing this policy.

As you might imagine, I received a variety of calls. One of my favorites was one Saturday the emergency line started ringing and again I yelled out "now fucking what?" I called the emergency line back and listened to the call. It was Marcus from building 6. Marcus, whom they called "Cus man" called the emergency line to get somebody over to the townhouse to repair his storm door immediately.

Now first of all, Cus man was not even a tenant! He was a house jumper illegally living there. He didn't think anything at all about calling to have the storm door (that he thought was his) repaired immediately. Storm doors had glass in them so I thought I had better get over there and address the issue. Also, he didn't leave a return phone number for me to call back to determine if it was an issue that needed immediate attention. Most of the time the tenants didn't leave their phone numbers or they rattled off their numbers so fast that I could not understand what the hell they said. Frustrating!

So I drove there that Saturday afternoon to inspect the door and determine if it needed immediate care. I walked up to the door and found that the bottom panel had been kicked out. I knocked on the inside front door and Cus man opened it. I asked, "what the hell happened?" He replied "I can't know! All of a sudden it got tat way." Of course I knew he was lying. I told him that this was not an emergency -- that he could have just kept the inside front door closed and waited until Monday to call in a maintenance request. He then gave me one of the most fucked up excuses why he needed the storm door panel fixed that day.

He said that he and his buddy were in the living room drinking beer and it was so hot in there that they wanted to open the storm door windows and the patio door and close the screen to get more airflow. I listened in complete amazement. This dumbass called me on the emergency line to get him and his buddy more airflow in a townhouse that he wasn't even supposed to be in the first place. I was fucking pissed. I then said "well…. You could have kept the storm door closed without the panel. It wasn't going to hurt anything." Then the dumbass actually said that it wasn't the panel he was worried about -- that it was the mosquitoes getting in and biting him. The funny thing about that fucked up statement was that I was beginning to realize that these types of situations were the norm within government housing.

Another one of my favorite emergency calls was about their complaints that the townhouse/apartment was too cold and that they had the thermostat "turned all the way up and it still was cold!" Remember, they would leave a message on the emergency line and talk so fast I could not understand them when they recited their phone number. However, I could understand when they gave their building number and apartment/townhouse number. This meant I was required to go there and address the issue.

The townhouses and apartments had water heat. Each unit had a valve that opened and closed that was connected to a thermostat in the dining room that controlled the heat in the household. On occasion, the valve would be stuck open or closed and needed to be replaced. That was a legitimate call. However, I would receive calls all of the time that the household was too cold. I would immediately go to these calls because I didn't want anyone (especially the kids) to be cold.

The first "too cold" call I went on was a lady named Tameca. She was a very nice lady. I knocked on the door and she opened and welcomed me in. She said that her heat wasn't working good enough and asked me to fix it because her baby was cold. The first thing that I noticed was that it was hot in the house. So I went to the thermostat. I noticed that she had it turned all the way up to 90 degrees. The thermostat read that it was 82 degrees in the apartment. I thought, 'are you kidding me? It's damn hot in here.' I asked Tameca to come to the thermostat and read it for me. She looked at it and said "it say it 82 in here but I got it up to 90. Why it only 82?" I replied that the furnace heats all of the townhouses and it can only put out so much heat. It was regulated and would cost a fortune to let everybody keep it at 90 degrees in their house.

I explained to her that it didn't matter if you turn the thermostat all the way up. It will only support so much heat and that's it. I could tell that she didn't like that response. I also told her that the state law for supplying heat was nothing below 67 degrees. She replied "67? That's fucked up!" Unfortunately, I received calls like this all of the time.

One evening after work, I took my shower and prepared a steak and shrimp dinner for my significant other and just sat down to begin our dinner together when the emergency line began ringing. We looked at each other and she saw the disqust on my face. I said "what the fuck now!" I listened to the message and then played it back for my significant other. She listened in dismay. The message was that I needed to get to the complex as soon as possible. There had been a shooting and a patio glass door had been shot out and I was required to secure the apartment.

I arrived to find 5 police cars surrounding an apartment and another car at the apartment that was shot up. I asked the police what was going on. They said that apparently the tenant in build 2 apt#12 had stolen a lot of marijuana from a tenant in building 3 apt#11. And apparently the tenant in #11 found out that the tenant in #12 was responsible. I said that's D'marco in #12 and they called him Pigskin and he's not a tenant but had been living there for over a year with his baby mama. The police said that the tenant in #11 found out that Pigskin and a couple of his friends coaxed the guy out of #11 and Pigskin went in and grabbed the pot and took off. I relayed to the police that the suspect in #11 was not a tenant and I heard through the grapevine that he was the tenant's brother and she was afraid of him.

The police said the reports are that the subject went to Pigskin's apartment to retrieve his pot. They said he pounded on the steel door and tried to break it down but was unsuccessful. He then returned to his sister's apartment and retrieved a pistol and proceeded to Pigskin's to get his pot back.

The report said that the suspect was seen yelling up to Pigskin's apartment warning Pigskin to throw his pot down to him or else. He didn't receive a response so he began firing his pistol through the glass panel next to the glass door. We counted six holes in the walls when we finally entered. He shot out the glass panel that is the same size as the glass patio door with 6 bullet holes throughout the apartment.

The police and detectives began their investigation. They immediately surrounded apartment #11 where the alleged shooter was staying. They soon discovered the shooter was not there. They determined he fled the scene.

So here was the aftermath: 6 bullet holes in the walls, the patio glass pane completely shot out, everyone living in an around the complex on edge and police and detective vehicles surrounding the neighborhood. All for a bunch of damn pot!

The investigators cut the bullet holes out of the walls leaving 6 inch by 6 inch holes. I had to find some plywood to cover the opening by the patio door which was around 4 feet by 6 feet and install it to provide the tenants with safety. It took us a couple of hours to complete the job.

The following day I had to order the replacement glass which was going to take at least 2 weeks to arrive. After a couple of weeks I was summoned to Pigskin's apartment on a maintenance request. I knocked on the door, yelled 'maintenance" and Pigskin opened the door and invited me in. His baby mama who lived there started yelling at me about the glass panel. She yelled "when is that glass gonna get fixed?" I replied "as soon as it gets here. We had to special order it." She started raving that it looked "ghetto" and to hurry up. I had to laugh. She asked me why I was laughing. I replied "if you don't want the place to look ghetto, then tell Pigskin not to steal a man's pot that has a gun!" She looked at Pigskin and started yelling at him. I had to intervene. I asked Pigskin if I could talk to him man to man. He shook his head yes. I told him that I see him around the complex talking to his friends and the kids that are always running around. I said "Pigskin! I see how you interact with people and I think you are smart and a born leader so why aren't you in college?" He replied that he didn't have the money for school. I told him that was a copout and that there was plenty of assistance out there for him. His baby mama said "I told you that dumb ass!" I then said that if he was interested I would help him find assistance for schooling. He said he would think about it. unfortunately he never got back to me. I feel as if I failed him.

One night after hours, I just went to bed and closed my eyes and the line started ringing. My normal reaction was "Fuck! Now what!" It was

57

a call from a really nice lady that lived in a 2-bedroom apartment. Her toilet was plugged. I knew I had to go there because the 2-bedroom apartments only had one toilet. This lady who we'll call Nancy was a sweet lady that was extremely overweight and had a hard time getting around. She explained to me the toilet had always acted up this way. I said let's take a look. Now imagine that you were just getting to sleep when you had to get up, get dressed, take a cold car to your job and unplug a toilet filled with crap and used toilet paper. I unpluged it and wished her a pleasant rest of the evening.

I was walking to my office one day when this tenant named Shekeia approached me to tell me that there's a hole in he living room wall and if I would fix it. I said sure. I asked her how that happened and she replied "my boyfriend did it". I asked her why? She replied "he got mad and instead of hitting me he hit the wall". I said ok I guess that is better than hitting you. So I went to Shekeia's apartment to inspect the damage. She wasn't there so I let myself in and discovered 21 holes the size of baseball all over the dining and living room walls! I started laughing. You see, eventually as a maintenance person you would find these situations comical. Getting angry was counterproductive and could drive you crazy.

I called my maintenance partner and asked him to assist me. On my way to her townhouse I was approached by another tenant who confided in me that Shekeia put those holes in the walls. While we were repairing the holes, Shakeia came back to observe us. I told her that we had to have a talk. She seemed scared. I told her that someone told me that she did this. I said "I'll tell you what, if you tell me the truth, I won't charge you for the damage. However, if you lie to me, it's $20 a hole!" She looked down at her shoes and said "ok it was me." I asked her why? She said she was mad at her boyfriend and couldn't contain herself. I thanked her for admitting it and said no charge this time but this time only. I said "one more thing, what did you use to make the holes?" She said she used the bottom of a wine bottle. I left with a big smile on my face.

One afternoon, I had just returned from one of our properties and I noticed a gentleman in the parking lot dressed in all black and gold pants and black and gold coat. I thought it was a cool look because I like it when people add a little flare to their wardrobe style. Anyways, he was walking through the parking lot when out of nowhere a very large woman ran up to him and started hitting him. He began to protect himself by whaling on her too. They exchanged verbal abuses and continued to swing at each other. After a few moments of that, they stood almost toe-to-toe and started spitting at each other's face. I went into the office where the staff all continued to watch.

While they were spitting on each other and exchanging verbal unpleasantries, another very big lady jumped on the guy and began hitting him. All of a sudden we witnessed the three of them all tied up like a twister game and they inched their way in between two parked cars. At this point we still found this comical. Then I said to Karen, ok we have to call the police now. She asked why. I said come over here and look what the guy has. She picked up the phone and called 911. She told the operator that we had a dispute in the parking lot between one male and now three females fighting and the guy had a 13 inch butcher knife he was holding up in the air and to please hurry.

I was very surprised that the guy didn't use the knife while the three women were whaling on him and spitting in his face. The police arrived with 5 squad cars, guns drawn and demanded the guy drop the knife. It took him awhile, but he threw the knife into the field. The police arrested all of them. I gave the guy credit for not using the knife while experiencing a beat down by three very angry women. However, what the fuck was he doing walking around with a butcher knife in the first place?

One morning I came into work to find a police car in the parking lot next to our office. I entered to find Karen and two police officers reviewing our surveillance tapes. They asked me if I knew a black gentleman known as Casanova. I told them that I know what he looks like however had no idea who he was and I had not seen him running around here in awhile. I said that I was sure that he was a house jumper. A house jumper lives in an apartment until they overstay their welcome and get kicked out. Then they slither their way into another tenant's apartment until they get kicked out again. It's almost like – rinse and repeat, rinse and repeat. LOL.

Well, the police were viewing the previous night's surveillance searching for three separate women all brandishing weapons. Evidently, these women were fighting over Casanova with baseball bats. On one surveillance tape, a woman was pounding on another woman's door with a baseball bat yelling "come on out here you fucking bitch! I is gonna mess you up bitch!" Again, I had to laugh. They all ended up getting evicted. I was pissed -- because Casanova couldn't keep it in his pants, now we had to renovate three apartments.

We had just completed renovating a townhouse for a new resident and her children. Her name was Chantoya and she and her kids had just moved in when we received a call to the office about strange noises coming from the house. The caller (Joan) lived right behind Chantoya and entered a complaint of noises happening at all hours of the night.

I went to Joan's home to field the complaint. She said that right after Chantoya moved in that she could hear loud thumps, yelling and crashes through her firewall which separates the townhouses. Joan said that the night before her pictures on her separation wall fell off. She claimed that something hit the wall behind her so hard that it shook her wall and should be investigated. I thanked her for the information and promised that it would be investigated.

I felt given the information that it might be an issue with severe safety issues. I knocked on the door several times with no response. I heard voices in the house, however, unfortunately we were not allowed to enter without a 12-hour notice. I posted the door with a 'notice to enter' and promptly returned the next day.

I entered the following day with the cleaning lady. I brought the cleaners for support and to serve as witnesses just in case there was trouble. Nobody answered the door so we entered with trepidation and a camera. We discovered the house to be a complete disaster. We also discovered at least 7 holes in the walls ranging from the size of a fist to the size of a folding chair. Obviously, someone was throwing somebody around and punching walls.

Now, they had just moved in! Usually, tenants get acclimated to the building and surrounding neighbors before they start tearing the place apart. Nevertheless, Joan and I took some pictures and reported this to the office. In the office, Karen had Joan post a lease violation for excessive noise and left it at that. I put together a plan to fix the holes and have a chat with Chantoya about the noise and holes.

I approached Chantoya a couple of days later and asked her "what the hell went on here?" She replied, "my baby daddy came in and started throwing me all over the place and he hit the walls with his fist hard!" I asked if she invited him here. She replied "no way! I don't want his ass here -- that's why I moved here from Chicago. He followed me and forced his way in." I asked her if she called the police. She said that if she called the "po-po he would probably hurt her real bad." She said she was scared to death of him.

As more time was spent in this maintenance position, I realized that this is common behavior that pervades within government housing. All we could do was to monitor the townhouses, repair the holes and other damages without charge, and hope for the best --- especially for the kids.

We received a call from our local police that an Asian tenant in building 2 broke into a townhouse and kidnapped his own kids and was on the loose. We had to chuckle because we knew this person and never thought he would ever do something like this. His name was Cho and in my opinion, seemed to be a very nice, calm individual that loved his kids.

The police said that Cho and his wife had a fight and he grabbed the kids and took off in his mini van. There was an APB (all points bulletin) out for his arrest. Later that day, the police called and said they located Cho driving on the highway and pursued him for about 8 miles before he finally pulled over. Cho was in deep trouble. The police returned the children to their mother and threw Cho in jail.

Cho finally got out of jail and moved in with his wife and kids a few months later. His wife moved to Michigan shortly after that leaving Cho with the townhouse and the kids.

I was entering our parking lot one morning preparing to start my day when I noticed a blanket over a patio door in an upper apartment. I thought, now what. I reached the office and sure enough, the police were there waiting for the office to open. I greeted them with a smile on my face knowing there was a problem. They usually had the same demeanor especially with me because I had become so used to "stupid acts" almost every day that I just shook my head and chuckled.

The police said that they received a call from the tenant in building #5 apartment #12 late last night that her baby daddy scaled the wall, jumped on to her balcony and broke the glass patio door to gain entry. Luckily for the tenant and the children, they had a feeling that this was going to happen and they all stayed with a friend in a different building.

The police report stated that a witness saw the suspect at around 1am scale the outside wall to gain entry into #12. He broke the glass patio door to discover that nobody was there and proceeded to let himself out the front door and took off.

When we talked to the tenant she said that her baby daddy was out to get her for moving without telling him and that he was out to get her. She seemed petrified of him. We installed plywood over the patio door until a new door was delivered.

I am still to this day trying to figure out how he scaled the wall to gain access to the balcony. These criminal acts happened so often that I oftentimes shook my head and laughed at the criminals. I felt very sorry for the mothers and especially the children that had to witness this type of behavior.

CHAPTER 9

Unbelievable Issues

Issue: Puppies

This might be the longest chapter in this book. I have witnessed so many head shaking random acts of disrespect for: property, other tenants, management, government rules and regulations, the police, surrounding neighborhoods and the school systems. So many issues that it's difficult to know exactly where to start.

I am going to begin with my personal 2nd most disturbing experience and end this chapter with my most disturbing experience. Buckle up!

Second most disturbing experience: It was a weekend when the emergency line on my phone rang. Again I thought, "now fucking what?" It was a tenant that left a message for somebody to come help her with a problem that she found by the dumpster. The caller was crying and quite frantic! She did not leave a return number so I jumped into my car and hurried to the complex. All kinds of scenarios were racing through my head.

I arrived to find many people around the dumpster including the police and our local animal rescue unit. I was surprised to see so many tenants around the dumpster. Usually nobody wanted to get involved with other peoples' issues. They seemed to stay clear from the police when they were around.

I approached the police to find out what was going on. One of the officers asked me to be patient while they were gathering information. Finally, after a few minutes, they came by me to explain what was going on.

They said they received a call from one of the tenants that she was taking her garbage to the dumpster and could hear some strange noises in the dumpster. She told he police that at first it sounded like a wounded squirrel or raccoon. She was hesitant to look inside but did so anyways. She said she saw three white garbage bags that were moving and could hear whining and screeching coming from them. She ran and got her brother to check it out. She said that her brother pulled out the first garbage bag and opened it to discover a pitbull puppy that seemed blind and was in pain. He then pulled the other garbage bags out and found more pitbull puppies inside them. Three pitbull puppies altogether. All three were in pain and appeared to have a difficult time seeing.

While I was talking to the officer, I noticed another officer arresting one of our tenants. Her name was Anne. She lived in building #6 with her five and six-year-old boys. The police put the two boys in one squad car and Anne in the other. Animal Protective Services rushed the puppies to receive immediate veterinary care.

I locked up Anne's townhouse and searched for answers. I approached the small grouping of tenants to obtain any information I could. I was extremely concerned due to the heart wrenching condition of those poor puppies. They looked so frail and scared. I didn't gather any more information on top of what I already knew so I went to the office and wrote a small report of what happened and then returned home.

The following day was a Monday and I couldn't wait to get to work to find out more information. Karen and I waited to hear the police report with much anticipation. We both loved dogs. Finally an officer came in to give a comprehensive report around 10am.

We were shocked and angered to hear the specifics of the report. Karen almost started crying. Apparently, Anne had received 3 pitbull puppies from another tenant. It seemed that was the dog of choice in government housing. Anne was sleeping in her upstairs bedroom I the early afternoon. The two young boys were in the basement with the puppies. The boys told the police that the puppies were yelping too much and they wanted to stop them from making so much noise. So they said they poured bleach all over the puppies, shoved them into garbage bags, and threw them into the dumpster.

I said out loud "are you fucking kidding me?" I was extremely upset and so was Karen. It made me sick to my stomach. Karen immediately said that she would start the eviction process. The officer said that the boys were with family members and that Anne would be released from jail soon. We also asked for an update of the puppies' condition. We were told they were going to be ok but needed treatment for the bleach to their eyes and their fur. This experience was troubling and hard to forget. We ended up evicting Anne and she was subsequently put on probation. Anne and her boys moved in with family and part of her probation prohibited her from owning any animals. To this day, I remain upset about this incident.

Issue: Parking lot stupidity

One morning when I just got to work, I drove into the parking lot on my way to the office. I noticed several cars in the parking lot that didn't look recognizable. I didn't really know what to think. There were approximately 12 cars taking up spaces from our tenants. It didn't take long for the emergency line to start ringing with a field of complaints about the cars. One of the cars was parked in a private spot for a tenant with special needs and those tenants weren't happy.

I immediately started knocking on doors to see if anyone knew who the owners were of these cars. I went to the building where a concentration of these cars were parked. The first door I knocked on was a tenant that was not happy with this new issue and confided in me that I should go ask Yanika who lived upstairs. I knocked on Yanika's door. She finally opened the door and said "oh hi." I asked her if she knew whose cars were parked all over the place in the parking lot. She replied, "they belong to my friend Calvin." I asked "all of them?" She replied "yes." She went on to tell me that Calvin was renting a small car dealership lot and got evicted and needed a place to take the cars.

I just started laughing. I asked her if Calvin had a phone and if so, to please get him on the line "right now." She got this individual on the line and I told him who I was and that the lot was private property and to remove the cars immediately or we would have them towed away. He started to argue and I just replied "you have 24 hours" and he hung up on me. I said to Yanika, "who the hell does he think he is? He's got a lot of nerve to think he can use a private parking lot to park his cars on!" I shook my head and said "Jesus Christ!" and left.

I had gone to the hardware store and when I returned to the office, the office girls said that I missed the fireworks. They said Calvin came in with a baseball bat looking for me. I told them he was fucking lucky I wasn't there. He'd be in jail right now. It took him and his cronies a week to get those pieces of crap out of our parking lot. We found out that Calvin had lost the keys to these cars so we had to laugh while watching these guys breaking into the cars to try to get them started. Also we were experiencing a cold blast that made it even funnier to watch.

Issue: One Million Bugs

I was passing through a hallway in our apartment building when I noticed an extension cord plugged into an outlet in the hallway and went into apartment #1. I knocked on the door and Adam opened it and greeted me. I asked what he was doing while pointing to the cord. He said that he hadn't paid the electric bill in over 5 months and they shut his power off. I told him that he couldn't do that and he had 48 hours to get it taken care of. Three days later the cord was still there. I went to the basement and turned off the circuit breaker to that outlet.

Let me give you some background on Adam and his roommate Bill. Adam was a nice person in his twenties. I had never met his roommate, but evidently Adam and Bill were friends who had applied for government housing together. The HUD rule was that any two people could apply for a two-bedroom apartment if they didn't have enough income for non-government housing. Adam had found a very part time job and did report it to the office. His rent was $12/month. These two boys were very able individuals. They were using the system to have a party place for free. They were lazy. I knew all of this because I personally knew Adam and his parents. Note: Even though his rent was $12/month, he was four months behind in rent when I discovered the extension cord plugged into the hallway outlet.

About two months after I turned the circuit breaker off, we received a call that Adam's apartment had a bad odor to it. Also, we had reports that he moved out. I posted the door for an inspection and returned the following day. What I found made my stomach turn.

The cleaning lady and I entered the apartment and we were almost knocked down by the stench. We looked at each other with a 'can't fucking believe it' look on our faces. The first thing we noticed while holding our breath was that Adam apparently had a dog. The carpet in the living room was soiled with dog shit and piss. The dog also tore a hole in the carpet the size of a lounge chair. There was a huge ugly bar built from 2 x 4's and unpainted plywood. The bar was covered with empty pizza boxes, empty booze and beer bottles, cigarette butts, and leftover moldy food. It was disgusting.

We proceeded into the kitchen. The stove was covered in everything imaginable and so greasy everything stuck to it. The counter tops were buried in everything from old moldy food to dirty dishes. There were so many dirty dishes, pans and small appliances in the sink that if you didn't know where the sink was, you couldn't find it. I looked under the sink and discovered that the drain plumbing was completely gone. The top of the cabinets had at least 50 empty bottles of vodka and tequila. The cabinets were also filled.

My personal favorite: We opened the refrigerator door and almost passed out! The nasty stench was so bad the cleaning lady ran into the living room. It was filled with food so moldy we couldn't identify what it was. The refrigerator and freezer had thousands of weevils – tiny black bugs. There were so many of these black bugs they actually stained the plastic inner lining. This perfectly good refrigerator was destroyed. Remember, the power had been turned off for a couple of months during a hot summer.

We continued our inspections into the bedrooms. We noticed everything was still left there except for clothes in the closet and dressers. They left beds, all of the nasty stained bedding, beat up dressers and end tables, old smelly clothes, ashtrays full of butts and a host of all kinds of what we would call "just plain crap." Also typically, the blinds were destroyed and the windows were covered with old blankets and towels.

We continued into the bathroom. Oh my God! Nasty can't even explain it. Everything was covered in black film. The bathtub walls had several tiles missing and a hole in the tub surround wall. The sink was plugged and a great big turd left for us as if there were saying "take THAT mother fuckers! Ha ha!"

Here were two boys that not only used the system but abused the property and thought nothing of it. I knew this because I ran into Adam at Wal Mart and asked him why he left it that way. He just shook his head and said "not my problem."

It took many resources and a lot of time and taxpayer money to rehab that apartment.

Issue: Lazy and entitled.

I was in the office and Karen asked me to come in. She said that she received a letter from a doctor stating that Shanice (in building #2 apartment #3) was eligible for a PRIVATE parking spot right in front of her building due to a leg ailment. I replied, "what? She is lying right through her teeth. I had never seen her limping or in pain. She wants a private spot?" Karen said it didn't matter what we saw or thought. The HUD rule was that if anyone got a doctor to sign a document stating special conditions for a private spot, we had absolutely no recourse. We had to comply. I mentioned to Karen that this was going to open up a "huge can of worms." Once everyone saw this, there would be more scams to come.

The request to have a private parking spot meant that we had to order a special sign on a steal post indicating that this spot was private for this particular apartment. We were required to cement the steal post in the ground or black top and had a small time-frame to do this. We had several more scam requests after the first sign went up!

Issue: Cabin up North?

We had a call that our tenant Trista had moved out of her townhouse. I did an inspection and discovered that all of her things were still there and the place was clean. It appeared to me that she wasn't living there but her things were there and nothing looked out of place.

We finally discovered through her friend that Trista moved to back Chicago but wanted to keep this townhouse for a vacation home. However, Trista claimed she was taking care her parents that just happens to be in hospice together at the same time. We waited for a couple of months to see if she would return. She had not.

After an exhausted search, Karen finally got in touch with her through the phone. Trista still claimed that her parents were still in hospice. When Karen relayed that to me I had to laugh. Karen gave her one month to move back in or we would start the eviction process. Trista became enraged. Trista threatened to call HUD and make a formal complaint against Karen. Karen replied "Go ahead. I am following HUD rules."

Trista did follow through with her threat and placed a formal complaint against Karen. It went nowhere. Karen filed for an eviction. Trista decided to come back to the complex to save her townhouse. She moved back in but only for a short time. She decided to bring some of her relatives up and move in with her to give the place some action. She went back to Chicago a month later purposely leaving people that were not on the lease. We were stuck. We knew that she was using this townhouse for a getaway from Chicago from time-to-time. There was nothing we could do about it. Our hands were tied. We could not prove that she was not living there. One of her friends confided in us that Trista lived in another government housing project in Chicago and was using the system to have 2 places to live since they were both basically free. Trista kept working the system until she finally turned in her keys 3 years later.

Issue: Time for a Christmas Tree

We received a notice from HUD for an impending inspection for all apartments and the grounds and common areas in late November. We usually received a 30 day notice. This meant the maintenance department had to do apartment inspections and inspections around the complex. The office was responsible for all paperwork including lease renewals, all incoming monies, all outgoing bills etc. It was very nerve racking to all of us.

I started my inspections immediately. I started with the apartments and townhouses. I started there because we had many tenants and their families that destroyed things faster than we could fix them. Remember, we couldn't charge them for damages so most of them just plain didn't care. So I entered every apartment and townhouse and conducted an inspection. I then put a list together of the damages and hit the ground running every day to make repairs until the day of the inspection.

While conducting my inspections, I entered a townhouse in building 4. The tenant was a single woman named Sherry with three children all under the age of 12. She greeted me with a smile and asked how I was doing. I said that I was ok and would be better when the inspection was over. She said "yeah, I get it – people around here can be nasty." I replied, "if you only knew." I also said "not all of them – everyone around here is very nice to me. I just wish they would take better care of their homes."

Sherry invited me to start the inspection. The first thing I noticed was that the patio doors were covered with a dark blanket. I asked her why the blanket was over the patio door when she had vertical blinds. She told me that her ex-boyfriend was stalking her and the kids and was trying to peek through the blinds. I said 'ok' but I had to pull the blanket off temporarily for the inspection. She said that was ok.

I pulled the blanket off to get more light in the living room and could not believe my eyes. Remember, it was a few days before Christmas. There on the living room wall was a 6-foot high 4-foot wide Christmas tree that was colored on the wall by crayons!! I promptly asked what that was? Sherry replied "I didn't have a tree so we colored one on the wall." I understood the desperation, but now I had to get some oil-based polyurethane paint to cover the tree art, let it dry for two days, and paint over that with our regular paint before the inspection. Sherry apologized with a sad look on her face. I told her I would wait until after Christmas to do the repair. She thanked me. I asked her to never do that again and I would find her an imitation tree for next year.

Issue: Why Clean?

I continued inspecting and went to building #2 to an apartment where the tenants consisted of a dad and mom with their two boys. They had lived there for over 10 years.

They were a very nice family and respectful. When I walked in, I noticed that the entire place looked as if I was in a "Hoarding" episode on TV. There were only paths to follow to get to the bedrooms and bathroom. The living room was completely full of musty furniture, old stereos, grungy chairs, living room tables covered with everything imaginable. The TV looked as if it was a black & white set – however, it was color to my surprise. Everything was covered in years of dust. The paint on the walls was faded and moldy in some spots.

I went into the kitchen and everything was covered in extreme grease. The stove was ready to burst into flames the next time it was used. The sink was encased with a thick film of dirt and grease and of course, full of dirty dishes. The counters were covered with old appliances and food. On top of the refrigerator was moldy bread – seemed to be a norm at this complex.

In the bathroom I noticed more dirty film over everything. The walls and ceiling were full of mold. The toilet was black in most spots and smelly. The sink was plugged spotty with toothpaste, makeup and things that I couldn't identify. The mirror was extremely dirty and streaky.

I moved to the bedrooms. Again, they were jammed-packed with old clothes, dressers, etc. The walls also had mold all over them in certain spots. I asked the tenants how long had all of this been going on. They said two years. I told them that this was a dangerous situation and needed to be addressed immediately.

I kept thinking.... I would love to come in here and start cleaning, organizing, and throw out all of the junk that had not been used in years. I felt bad for them. But then I had to come to the realization that they live like this because they want to. I was also concerned for the two boys. I felt this living model would become ingrained in them and that it would follow them to their own places someday.

I explained to them that they had to clean the place up. I asked them to get rid of the stuff they didn't use anymore. I tried to explain that hoarding all of this stuff was a fire hazard. They looked at me seemingly confused. They replied that they had lived this way for years and that nobody from the company ever said anything. I told them that whoever let this slide before me didn't have their best interest at heart. I gave them one week to rectify the issues.

I returned the following week for an inspection. I did notice a pathetic effort to clean and organize on their part. However, they just moved their things from one side of the room to the other. The years of dirt and dust in every room on the appliances, sinks, toilet and bathtub all had swirly marks all over them. It exemplified their effort to comply. I decided to ignore the apartment and not to criticize their choice of living conditions. I just prayed their apartment didn't make the list of REAC inspections next time around.

Issue: Pull that toilet!

I was continuing with my inspections when I received a call from the office to hurry over to building #4 townhouse #12. Karen said the police just did a raid there and they needed a maintenance person immediately. I asked her why? It didn't make sense to me. She said she was unaware of the raid and that I needed to get there right away. That the police were waiting for me. I said ok, I am on my way.

I approached the townhouse and noticed 3 police cars, 2 unmarked detective cars and a swarm of police waiting for me. I thought that this was going to be a new experience and somewhat of an adventure.

I walked up to the townhouse and a police officer asked me to go to the main bathroom to talk to the head detective of the M.E.G. unit. I went to the bathroom and the detective asked me to pull the toilet. He said that when the police knocked on the door, they heard a toilet being flushed. He explained that there might be drugs in the drain. He then asked me if that would be possible. I replied "probably not." I explained that the waste goes past the trap in the toilet and straight down the 4 inch drain pipe right to the road. However, I agreed to pull the toilet. I then pulled the toilet, took it outside, turned it upside down on the grass for the detectives to inspect for drugs. They didn't find anything and all of them left. They did thank me but left me to clean up the mess and reinstall the toilet. Fun times!!!!

Issue: Know when to shut up!!!

I was on a maintenance call to repair a hole in a wall in the foyer of a tenant who liked to keep me informed on scrupulous behavior around the complex. This tenant is named Nichele. She was very nice and seemed to care about the health and safety of her 4 kids. While I was assessing the hole which was the size of a bedroom window, Nichele asked me if I had heard about Shawanda. Shawanda lived in a townhouse with her abusive baby daddy and three kids next to Nichele. I replied "No! Now what did she do?" Nichele just started laughing and said "that crazy bitch got herself arrested two times in less than an hour!"

I asked what happened. Nichele said that Shawanda and Edwina got into it last night. I asked what happened. Nichele said that Shawanda stormed over to Edwina's house and started pounding on the door saying "open this fucking door bitch!" Nichele said that Shawanda was not going to leave until she "said her mind out." Nichele explained the confrontation to me this way – Shawanda was made because one of her kids came home complaining that he was bullied by one of Edwina's kids.

Shawanda went there to settle the score. She pounded on the door until Edwina finally came out. The two of them got into an extremely heated and very loud exchange of insults. They went at it for a long time – neither one relenting. Finally after 30 minutes of constant screaming threats, the police arrived -- obviously, somebody called them.

The police approached the fighting women and made several attempts to split them up and calm them down. Nichele said that Edwina finally calmed down but Shawanda was "out of control." The police warned Shawanda several times to calm down or she would be arrested and taken downtown to sit in jail. She would not calm down and started targeting the police screaming – "Fuck you po po! Black lives matter! Black lives matter! You racist! You racist! Get away from me." The police warned her one more time to calm down or she would be arrested. She would not listen. They finally arrested her and took her downtown and put her in jail. She received a citation for disorderly conduct and was released.

Nichele said that you would think that Shawanda would have learned her lesson and kept her big mouth shut. Nichele said "Nope! She gets out of jail and first thing she does is starts pounding on Edwina's door blaming her for getting arrested." Nichele said Shawanda was even more enraged if that was even possible. Well.... here came the police again. They arrested her for the second time in less than an hour of arresting her the first time. They put her in the squad car and all you could hear was "Fuck you! You racist pigs! Let me out!" Shawanda ended up spending the night in jail.

Issue: Don't give a shit

I was working at my desk around 11am when I noticed a huge U-Haul truck backing up to a townhouse on the grass to help a move-out. This was disturbing because they didn't get permission to drive on the grass and the ground was soaked due to heavy rain the night before.

I decided not to confront them because the damage was already done and they were moving anyway – so what was the point? There were three guys helping load the U-Haul which took about two hours. I kept an eye on them because one never knows what could happen – and I was right.

After they loaded the truck and prepared to leave, they decided to take a different route over the grass. They proceeded to the parking lot right in front of the office. It seemed they didn't care if we noticed them driving on the soaked grass causing deep tire trenches. I noticed them laughing and seemingly having a good time – until they got stuck. I began laughing inside the office and invited the office girls to join me in watching these idiots try to get unstuck.

They worked on it for at least 30 minutes. They stood back reviewing the situation – all scratching their heads. I was still laughing. Finally I decided to approach them to see if I could help. I drove up in my gator and asked who was in charge of this operation. They all looked at each other and just shrugged their shoulders. Inside I was still laughing. I said I would go get some plywood for them to place under the wheels for traction. They just looked at me. Not one of them thanked me! I grabbed some plywood and returned. I said "this would help, but if it doesn't you might have to unload the U-Haul to make it lighter to get out of the deep ditches the tires caused." They looked at each other saying "fuck this shit."

They proceeded to place the plywood under the wheels and rock their way out. It wasn't working. After about an hour of this, they started unloading the U-Haul. They finally worked the truck off the now muddy grass onto the parking lot. They loaded their stuff back onto the truck and took off.

I went to retrieve the muddy plywood. When I drove up I noticed they conveniently left a bunch of stuff behind on purpose. The items included a gallon jar of old cooking grease, an ironing board, some pots and pans, pillows and an old bath towel.

I was left thinking --- they drove on the soaked lawn without permission, caused huge trenches in the lawn, ruined the grass, got stuck, had help from me, left a bunch of crap for us to pick up and take to the dumpster and took off without any one of them saying "sorry about the grass or thank you for the help!" I guessed they just didn't give a shit!

Issue: Before you die.

I was conducting an inspection in building #1 townhouse #6. The tenant was a gentleman in his seventies that had been in government housing for around 15 years. His name was Tommy. Tommy, in my opinion, was a very nice person with some major health problems. I would take ten minutes (on occasion) to visit with him and listen to his stories of when he used to be a rebel. He told me one time that he shot a guy in the Sierra desert and left him to die. That's the type of character he was.

While doing his inspection, I noticed that his basement was filled to the rafters with a bunch of old junky furniture and other stuff. Also, his two unused bedrooms upstairs were also filled to the ceilings. I asked Tommy where all of this stuff came from. He said that his son got kicked out of his apartment and he was storing his stuff here. I told Tommy that all of this stuff was a fire hazard and it had to be removed. He agreed. I said that I would be back in a month to verify that this stuff had been removed.

I returned several times to see if anything had been done to remove the stuff. He kept reassuring me that soon his son would come pick the stuff up. Fast forward three more months and nothing was even touched. I asked him to be honest with me and tell me why nothing was being done to remove all of the junk. He told me his son was still looking for a place to live and then he would pick up his stuff. Tommy then informed me that he had cancer and might not make it much longer. I gave him my condolences.

We then had a heart-to-heart talk about his life – including his kids. He told me that he was extremely disappointed in his kids – especially his son. I asked him if he died, what was going to happen to his personal belongings. He said his son would take care of it. I asked him to contact his son and have him start getting all of the stuff organized – to start throwing things in dumpsters that he didn't want. Tommy said he'd contact his son.

Three months after that conversation, Tommy died. I was saddened by the news.

After Tommy died, I entered his apartment expecting to see some of the stuff gone. Not so. The place was still filled to the rafters and ceilings. I ran into Tommy's son and asked him to start removing his stuff. His son took the TV, the only item of value, and left! Apparently, his son was living there illegally. I changed the locks and prepared to rent a dumpster to remove two households of crap. After I changed the locks, I noticed Tommy's son living in his pickup truck in our parking lot. Tommy had assured me that before he died, he would get all of this stuff out so we wouldn't have to deal with it. I don't think he meant it.

Issue: I don't like this floor

In continuing my constant inspections, I entered Shantice's townhouse for a quick inspection. I knew it would be quick because Shantice usually kept her townhouse organized and clean. I would always commend her for the way she kept her place. I would actually thank her almost every time I had a maintenance request. She would always reply by saying that she had seen some of the ways her friends around the complex lived. She'd remark "some of these people nasty!" I always replied "well… they have kids to run after" and I would just leave it at that.

In conducting the inspection I noticed the dining room and kitchen floor looked different. When one entered the townhouses from the front door, they'd come upon a foyer that lead to a dining room, bathroom and kitchen. We always had tile flooring in these areas. Some of these areas had square tiles and some had sheet tile. What I noticed when inspecting Shantice's flooring was that she took it upon herself to go buy square tile and stick it on top of the already-tiled floor. I couldn't believe it. It took a professional to install a floor like that. There were corners, moldings, under heat registers and floor striping to cut around and go under. It was kinda shocking. Shantice only had enough sticky tiles to do about half the floor.

I decided not to say anything to her against my better judgment. If I had addressed the situation, I would be responsible to fix it. I decided to take a chance that HUD would not see the floor.

About 4 months later, I had a maintenance request for a bathtub drain that was plugged. I knocked on the door and Shantice invited me in. I couldn't believe my eyes! She had covered her tiles with different tiles! Now I really had to talk to her about it. I asked her why she took it upon herself to retile the floor twice. She replied "because I didn't like the patterns, but now I got a pattern I like." I said that it was a lease violation and she could be in trouble for doing that. She looked at me in a confused manner. I told her that I wouldn't say anything but not to do anything like that again.

Issue: Don't kick the door down

In continuing with my inspections due to an impending REAC inspection, I knocked on apartment #12's door in building #3. Tammy, a very young mother of a two-year-old answered. I told her that I was there to do a pre-inspection of the apartment. She seemed a tad bit frightened of an inspection, however she let me in.

I immediately noticed a young man sitting on the couch. I said hello. He just looked at me. I asked him politely "so what's your name?" He replied "I'm Deshawn" in a disrespectful tone. I told him that I was there to do an inspection and he said "do what you gotta do man." I knew that Deshawn was living there illegally and didn't want me to know -- but I knew.

I began the inspection. The apartment was messy. The windows and glass patio door were covered with blankets and towels. I asked Tammy to remove their window dressings while I was conducting the inspection. She obliged. Finally some light. The first thing I noticed was a hole in the living room wall the size of a beach ball. To me, this discovery wasn't a surprise as I had come to almost always expect this while doing inspections. It was common place around this complex. I continued. Then I noticed another hole in the wall the size of a baseball and/or a fist. I thought ok, not so bad. Then I noticed the bedroom door kicked in and hanging by a single screw. I said "what the hell happened in here?" Tammy jumped in and said that her baby was locked in and that Deshawn had to break in to get her out. I knew she was lying! Typically, the girlfriend becomes afraid of the baby daddy/boyfriend and locks herself in her bedroom. The baby daddy/boyfriend kicks in the door. It was my opinion that they did that to show who was boss and to not dare disrespect them.

I told both of them that I was coming back later that day to repair the door and warned Deshawn not to kick the door in again and that I was going to replace the locking door knob with a non-locking door knob so that this incident wouldn't happen again. He just looked at me with no response.

I returned that day to repair the door. I did repair the door, however was unable to install a non-locking door knob. I told Deshawn and Tammy that I was currently out of non-locking door knobs and that I ordered some for tomorrow's delivery. I said "I will be back tomorrow to replace the door knob and please do not kick in the door!" I asked Deshawn to call the office or emergency line if the child gets locked in again. He replied "gotcha boss" and proceeded to lay on the couch.

I returned the next day to install the non-locking door knob. I knocked on the door and Tammy opened it and had a scared look on her face. She noticed the new door knob and said that they had a problem. I said "don't tell me" shaking my head. She said that the child locked himself in again and that Deshawn had to kick the door in again. I looked at her and Deshawn and had everything within me not to get into Deshawn's face. I knew that they were lying. I said rather forcefully "you gotta be kidding me! Didn't I just yesterday instruct you not to kick in the door!" They just looked at each other. I was really pissed off!

I told them that I was going to fix it again and that I didn't believe them. Tammy seemed contrite but Deshawn seemed not to give a shit. I told them next time this happened, I would charge them to fix every single hole in the walls as well as kicked-in doors. Note: I was getting really good at fixing kicked in damaged doors and frames. Sometimes the doors had holes the size of basketballs – and I could fix them quickly.

Issue: "I want my floor fixed now!"

I was in the office going over my maintenance requests when we received a call from building #5 apartment #3. It was Amaya calling to complain about her kitchen floor right in front of her refrigerator. She was complaining that there were holes in the sheet tile. I said to Karen "Holes? We just installed a new floor in the kitchen and dining room a month ago."

Amaya was a tenant who was only there on weekends. She stayed with her mom in Chicago during the week and there was hardly any furniture in the apartment. I always wondered why she had an apartment here when she was hardly ever here. Nonetheless, I went to inspect the floor.

Amaya was out of town and gave her permission to enter. I entered and noticed holes in the new floor and scrape marks right in front of the refrigerator. I was confused. It appeared that she tried to move the refrigerator. This confused me. Why would she move the refrigerator? Normally, nobody moved their refrigerators unless something fell behind them. However, Amaya's apartment was pretty bare and there was nothing on top of the refrigerator to fall behind it.

I returned to the office and reported my findings. I told Karen that I could probably cut and paste the damaged area but was confused what happened. I asked her if she could get Amaya on the phone. Karen said she would try to reach her.

We finally reached her and asked what happened. She said that she had bugs by her refrigerator and she pulled it out to spray. I asked her why she didn't call us to help. She replied "I hate those nasty bugs and it was the weekend and nobody around here." She claimed that there was something stuck under the refrigerator but she needed to spray right away. I told her that she damaged the new floor. She replied "Don't care. Dem was nasty bugs and had ta go."

I knew that we couldn't charge her for the damages so I called an exterminator to eliminate the cockroaches that she brought in and fixed the floor. Again, on the tax payer's dime.

Issue: We just walk over it

I had a maintenance request to unplug an upstairs toilet in building #5. I usually stopped what I was doing to immediately tend to toilet issues. I did that in case I had to pull the toilet and snake it upside down to dislodge the object/objects causing the blockage. This process could be quite time consuming.

I entered the townhouse and noticed a huge pitbull sitting in the corner. I asked when they got the dog. They said they were aware of the no dog policy unless it was a service dog. They claimed that it was their son's dog and their son was staying with them temporarily. I said ok and proceeded to the upstairs bathroom. I noticed on the way up the stairs some rather large dog poop on a couple of the steps. I didn't say anything at that moment. I wanted to complete the task at hand.

I ended up pulling the toilet, turning it upside down, placing it in the bathtub and snaking it. I discovered that it wasn't human poop, it was huge dog poop. I cleaned it out and remounted the toilet to the floor. I proceeded to leave the bathroom when I stepped into a huge pile of dog crap just outside the bathroom door. It was all over my shoes. I yelled "AH!!! SHIT!!" I heard some laughing coming from downstairs. I cleaned off my shoes with what was left of the toilet paper which was not much.

I went downstairs and they all had smirks on their faces. The audience consisted of the mother Betty, who sat at the dining room table every day with her friend Mandy. They chain smoked cigarettes as if the surgeon general now said it was good for your health and smoke as many as you could afford to. Betty's son Danny was also there with his son, Brad. They all couldn't wait to hear how I was going to respond to stepping in the dog crap.

I responded "Danny! What the hell? Why is this dog crapping all over the place and why isn't anybody cleaning this up?" Danny said that the dog refused to go outside to do his business so they let him do it in here and clean it up when they had time. I replied "When you have time? Really?" He said "yeah, we just step over it until we have time to clean it up."

I said that I wanted it cleaned up immediately. I also gave them a warning to fix the problem by either getting rid of the dog or by taking it out on a regular basis to train him to do his business outside. I didn't feel confident they were even listening. Note: I genuinely liked the family, however, I just didn't get how they could live with dog crap all over the carpeting and other flooring.

Issue: Do you hear that?

I was mulling around the office when Karen asked me to come into her office. I went in and sat down and asked what's up? She said that she had a complaint call from a tenant in building #1 that she could hear live chickens or baby chicks through her adjacent walls. I started laughing. I said "Let me guess? It's the Asian family in #5." Karen replied "you guessed it." I said they probably won't answer the door if we go over there right now. Karen asked me to post their door with a 24 hour notice for inspection. I told her that they would probably move the animals if they knew in advance that we were conducting an inspection. Karen said that we have to follow protocol but this time she would assist me with the inspection.

I was surprised by that because Karen hated going into the field to conduct anything. However, I posted the door and we waited until the following day to enter.

The next day I asked Karen if she was up for it and not to worry. It would be an adventure for her. I said the family was very nice and extremely respectful. Note: Out of all the years I was there, I could recall Karen in the field 4 or 5 times. Anyways, we walked up to the door and Karen noticed that all of the blinds were closed. I told her that was normal around the compound. I knocked on the door and yelled "inspections!" A sweet older Asian woman opened the door and gestured for us to enter. We entered and headed down to the basement because that's where they usually kept their animals.

We inspected the basement and all we discovered was a distinctive smell. I told Karen that was a normal kind of smell in the basements of Asian tenants. We proceeded to the upstairs bedrooms and bathroom. I told Karen to look for blood splatter. She looked at me with disgust in her eyes. I mentioned that if they had chickens, they probably processed them in the bathtub. She replied "gross." We didn't discover any blood or splatter in the bathroom so we headed to the kitchen. We still didn't find any evidence of chickens being there. We were on our way out and said thank you when Karen said "do you hear that?" I stopped in my tracks and listened quietly. Karen said "Oh my God, it's coming from that basket over there!" We headed to the basket and asked the lady to open it. She complied and removed the cover. We looked inside and I got a big smile on my face and started scratching my head saying "No, no, no -- you can't have baby chicks in the apartment" to the lady.

Karen and I had all we could do not to laugh. I had to remember that this was a different culture from what I was used to. We had to remember not to judge. However, it was a lease violation to raise animals for food in the townhouses/apartments. I approached the lady and asked her if she spoke English. She looked at me and replied "little." I said "no, no, no" while shaking my head side to side. She replied "ok." That's all she said. We left and I told Karen that I would keep an eye on the townhouse.

Note: The Asian community that I had witnessed also liked to put huge fish tanks in their basements and raise Coy and other large fish such as Oscars. I never asked why or found out why -- I simply respected their culture.

Issue: A free box full of drugs

I had a call to inspect a townhouse that was experiencing a bug problem throughout the house. It was in building #4 townhouse #1. The tenant was a younger girl named Mindy living there with her two-year-old daughter. Her boyfriend Bruce, who was not on the lease, was also living there. I knew Bruce from somewhere but couldn't place him. I did remember that he was a troubled young man that had problems with drugs.

I went to conduct my bug inspection and noticed that nobody was home. I entered the townhouse to find the place was trashed. Holes in the walls, furniture disheveled, food left out, pots, pans, and dishes used but not cleaned, ceiling fan going full blast and a rancid smell permeating throughout the place.

I was standing in the dining room next to the living room. I turned on my flashlight to start my bug inspection when I noticed an army of tiny bugs leaping onto my legs. I was quite surprised. I wasn't sure what the hell these little bugs were so I called the exterminator. He said that it sounded like fleas and to get out of the apartment if they were aggressive. So I posted the door and scheduled his services for the following day.

The next day I went in to work and Karen informed me that Mindy and Bruce were in jail and I needed to open the door for the exterminator. I asked "both of them?" She replied "yup." Karen said that the police raided their townhouse because both of them went to the police drug drop-off box, broke into it, and stole prescription drugs. I asked her what a drop-off box was. She said it was a box for people to dispose of their drugs that they didn't use or need anymore. I said "are you kidding me? They actually went to the safety building and broke into the box right in front of their cameras? What a couple of dumb asses!" Karen replied "It also means that they are now going to be evicted."

Issue: It smells funny in here

I had a maintenance request come over my desk from a new move-in in building #2. It was from a new move-in that I did not conduct the initial inspection with. Usually, I conducted the move-ins with new tenants. They were required to complete an inspection sheet with any concerns they observed such as minor scratches in the floors or any other imperfections. If they saw something that should be corrected, they had to mark it on the sheet or they could be held accountable for the damages when they moved out. What they didn't know was that the government never held them accountable for any damages they caused.

So I went to introduce myself to the new tenant and address the request. I knocked on the door and this very young girl answered. I was very surprised to find out it was another tenant's daughter Abby. I said "Oh hi! What are you doing here?" She replied "This is my new place." I said "Oh ok. Well let's look at the oven." The request was that the oven wasn't working. I discovered that the cleaning lady forgot to turn the circuit breaker back on after she cleaned it. I flipped it and approached Abby to inform her that it was the circuit breaker.

Abby was sitting in the living room with a couple of her friends that appeared to be teenagers. They all had big smiles on their faces. There was also a 2 month old baby sitting in a baby chair. I asked who the baby belong to. Abby replied "That's my baby. That's why I have my own apartment." I said "Oh, that makes sense." I could definitely smell pot in the room and I said "It smells funny in here." They all looked at each other and started laughing. I told Abby that her oven was all set and said goodbye and left the apartment.

A little background about Abby. Her mother Carol had been living at the complex for over 3 years. Carol had two daughters and one son. Abby was the oldest and on S.S.I due to a mental disability. Carol was a zero renter – a tenant that paid zero rent due to zero income. She relied on her ex-boyfriend, the children's father, to pay child support so she could have a car and other things.

After I left Abby's apartment, I was shaking my head. How was it possible that Abby became pregnant, had the child, and now has her own apartment unsupervised? I was contemplating what action I should take to expose the fact that there was a 18 year-old girl surrounded by her teenage friends unsupervised and smoking pot in front of the newborn. I decided to place this issue in Karen's lap – the property manager. I usually didn't inform the office when I smelled pot because the police would not address pot smoking. They pretty much informed us that they would be there all of the time if they addressed pot smoking. They were more concerned with the harder drugs like crack, heroin, pills, etc.

Karen decided to give Carol a call and place it in her lap with the hopes she would supervise the situation. Three months later, Abby moved back in with her mom. And I was relieved.

Issue: Look what they did to my truck!

I was doing a rehab on an apartment when I was approached by a tenant in building #5. His name was Steve. He lived in a two-bedroom lower apartment with his wife Chrissy. They were, in my opinion, somewhat goofy but nice. They had a baby that was taken away from them by social services. Steve told me Chrissy was displaying bouts of severe depression during doctor visits. Social services was called and subsequently removed the child. I was relieved. There was something a little off about this couple. I did whatever I could to make them feel appreciated as tenants though because I liked them.

Well, one day I was walking through the hallway when Steve approached me with an angry demeanor on his face. Before I could say anything, he said rather loudly "Come outside and look what they did to my truck!" I asked who? He said those two assholes that lived right above him. I asked what was going on with those two up there as we headed outside to examine his truck. I was thinking on the way outside that Steve had just bought a really nice used truck and I was concerned for him.

We approached his truck and pointed out all of the tiny dents all over the back and side of the truck. I asked what the hell happened. There must have been 200 tiny dents. He said that last week he had a confrontation with Cornell, the upstairs tenant, about the loud music and partying that went on all hours of the night. Now Cornell and his friend (whose name I didn't know) were not even tenants. They got the apartment through Cornell's sister. She was fed up with the partying and moved out without informing the office. Steve said that she had moved out months ago. Steve said that he asked Cornell several times to keep it down. Steve said he finally called the police.

The police showed up and gave Cornell a warning. Steve said it didn't help but what it did was to make them angry so they sat on their upstairs balcony and shot up his truck with a BB gun. I asked him if he called the police. He said that he was now afraid of them and kept his mouth shut. I told him that he should have called the office with a formal complaint.

I immediately went to the office to inform Karen that there were two individuals living in an apartment illegally and that the true tenant moved out months ago. Karen decided to warn Cornell to move out or legal action would be taken. I was worried because Cornell's sister didn't give us written notice that she was moving. That would make Cornell and his friend "squatters" and it would be a battle to get them out. Fortunately, they moved. When I went to inspect the apartment after they moved to change the locks I found many containers for BB's. And of course, the apartment was trashed!

Issue: Three in one day?

I was conducting an inspection one afternoon when I entered a townhouse in building #3. This townhouse consisted of a mother named Nisha and her two children. She had a young boy around ten-years-old and a daughter around eight- years-old (sorry, didn't get their names). Anyways, they were very nice to me and I liked them. She also had her baby daddy living there illegally.

I began the inspection when the young boy looked at me and said "Mister, we had a problem with some doors." I replied "what kind of problems?" He said that he and his sister were playing when one of the doors fell upstairs. I knew right away that someone kicked in or broke the door. I immediately assumed that it was the baby daddy. The reason for my assumption was that this scenario was way too common around the compound. I asked him what happened. He said "me and my sis was playing and the door came off." I said ok, let's go to take a look and asked him to follow me.

We went upstairs and to my surprise, the bathroom door was hanging by a screw and two of the bedroom doors were hanging but ready to fall off. I became visibly angry. The boy appeared scared and said it was his fault. He said that his sister wouldn't let him in the rooms so he forced his way in. I asked him when he did this. He replied "yesterday." I said "three in one day!" He said yes sir. I said where's your mother? And he replied that she was sleeping. I asked him where his dad was? He replied "he not here." I kind of felt sorry for him. He seemed quite contrite. I told him that I was going to fix the doors and don't ever do that again. He nodded and went to the living room.

I did fix them that same day and had a little chat with his mom and warned her that I would be forced to charge her if this would happen again. She apologized. Note: After I retired from government housing, I kept in touch with my replacement. During one of my conversations with him, he asked me about that same apartment. He asked me if I ever had to fix any doors there. I started laughing hysterically. I told him that I had to fix 3 doors in one day. We both had to chuckle. I told him that the problem is that they are such a nice family and respectful it's hard to get mad at them. He agreed.

Issue: If you lie to me!

I was on a maintenance request concerning a leak under the kitchen sink in building #3 townhouse #12 when the tenant whose name was Shantice approached me to inform me that her bedroom door upstairs had issues. She asked me to look at it when I was done fixing the leak under the sink. I said I would. After I replaced a J-trap under the sink, I went upstairs to check out the door. I discovered that not only was the door off the frame, but the frame was missing! I thought, here we go again. Another door broken into. I called for her to come upstairs immediately.

I said "Ok Shantice. What the hell happened here?" She replied "my boyfriend was moving the bed in here and it fell on the door and broke it." I looked at her and uncharacteristically of me I replied "I don't believe you!" She tried to assure me that she was being honest. I wasn't buying it! I told her that I was coming back later that day to fix the frame and re-hang the door and to think about her answer.

I returned with the proper tools to fix the door later that day. I spent at least an hour on the door and was able to put it all back together. It was like a jigsaw puzzle but I was getting amazingly good at fixing doors. I then asked Shantice to come upstairs and look at the repaired door. She looked a little scared. I said to her in a stern voice "I don't believe your story that your boyfriend, who is not supposed to be living here anyway, was moving furniture and it fell on the door tearing off the door and the frame!" She looked at me with scared eyes and replied "that's what happened." I then replied "I will tell you what, if you tell me the truth what really happened, I will not charge you for fixing the door." She hesitated. She was afraid to tell me the truth. I told her not to be afraid, just tell me the truth or this will cost you $100. She hesitated again, took a deep breath, and said "ok my boyfriend did it." She said that she wouldn't let him in the bedroom and he broke the door down. I thanked her for telling the truth. I also told her to give her boyfriend a message from me. If he ever did something like this again, we would evict you – which means he wouldn't have a place to live. She said ok. I felt bad for her at that moment but I was satisfied that she got the message.

Issue: Two time's a charm

Mark and Kerry were a married couple with three young kids living in building #3 townhouse #1. They family had been living there for about two years. They were quiet and kept to themselves for the most part. Mark on occasion walked around the complex grounds almost every day. I suspect it was for exercise or just something to do.

I was conducting a maintenance request at their townhouse when Mark asked me what was the policy for tenants driving their mopeds on sidewalks. I explained to him that it was against the rules and I knew what he was talking about – the couple of guys who were joy-riding their mopeds on the sidewalks that were on the property. I told him that I had already brought this issue to Karen's attention. Mark asked me to give him a follow up report on the issue. He said that he was afraid that his kids could get hurt because the guys driving these mopeds didn't care who was in the way. He said "those guys speed around here and yell at people to get the fuck out da way."

Two weeks later Karen informed me that Mark and the family were moving and we had to prepare to rehab their townhouse. I asked her what their reason was for moving. She told me that Mark said that he approached the two guys riding their mopeds around and asked them to please not ride the mopeds on the sidewalks. Mark said that ever since then, the guys were harassing him and said that they would kill him if he didn't shut his mouth. Karen said that that scared him enough to leave. I told Karen that we failed Mark and his family by not taking care of the issue. She agreed. I then told her that one of the guys was Amaya's brother that had been living with her illegally and seemed to be causing all kinds of trouble around the compound. Karen replied "too late. They are moving."

My immediate reaction was anger. Now I had to rehab a townhouse just because these two idiots didn't give a shit about the rules even though they were living there illegally.

Now let's fast forward one year later. Mark and Terry approached Karen regarding moving back to the complex. Karen informed him that the two guys that had threatened to kill him and who had harassed him were now gone. She told Mark that one of the guys ended up in jail and the other moved back to Chicago and that they were banned from the property. Mark was very happy to hear that and applied for a new townhouse. He was granted a townhouse in a different building than the one they were living in before.

Mark and the family moved into building #6 townhouse #2. I welcomed them back and apologized for letting them down with the previous moped issue. He was gracious and said that it was ok and they were glad to be back.

About two months later Mark and Terry came into the office to place a complaint about their adjacent neighbor. Their complaint was that almost every night they smelled pot through the walls and it made them sick to their stomachs. Karen assured them that she would look into it.

Karen and I had a meeting about what our options were. I said that the police really didn't care about pot smoking and we needed to do something on our end. I said to Karen, first thing, is to give them a written warning. Then I would have a talk with them personally while conducting a maintenance request. I told Karen that the tenant likes me and maybe I can persuade her to have her friends smoke it in the basement or don't smoke at all. Also, I recommended to Mark to call the police when you smell it. I told Mark that the police will knock on their door – however, 99 percent of the time, the tenants wouldn't open the door. Note: something told me this issue would not be resolved. I was right – they gave notice to move again! When I heard that they were moving again, my first thought was --- now I have to rehab another townhouse due to misconduct. That's rehabbing townhouses three times!! First when they initially moved in, second when they moved out and third, when they moved for the second time.

Issue: Drugs caused the flood

In building #2, apartment #7 lived a family of three. The mom and dad were in their late 70's and experiencing major health issues. They lived there with their son, Jay. Jay was in his 50's and unemployed. However, Jay was a very nice person in my opinion. I really enjoyed helping this family when needed. The apartment they lived in was unfortunately messy, dirty, smelly and packed with old furniture. However, I would offer to clean their carpets when I had a spare hour or two.

During the two years that I knew them, the dad died and the mom went into the hospital with cancer. Jay told me that the doctors were not sure if she would survive the treatments. I was saddened.

I let Karen know about the situation and asked her if Jay was on the lease in case the mom passed away Karen said that he was and if she died, Jay would have that apartment for the rest of his life if he wanted it. I told her I would keep her posted.

A couple of months later, she died – leaving Jay with the apartment and everything in it.

About a month after she died, Jay was walking across the compound when two police officers approached him to arrest him for back child support. During the arrest they asked him if he had any weapons or drugs on his person to which he replied "no weapons, but prescription drugs." The police asked to see them and the pills were not in a prescription bottle. He was busted and taken to jail. We found out that he was going to be there for at least three months. Karen had no recourse but to evict him.

During the eviction process we were experiencing a cold snap. A Polar Vortex. We received several calls from tenants in Jay's building that the heat wasn't working. So I went to the boiler room and discovered that the circulating pump had failed. That meant that there was no hot water pumping through the registers in the apartments. I called our heating guy to let him know right away. He said that it would take several hours to get a pump and install it. He also said that with the Polar Vortex upon us, that his phone was ringing off the wall. I said to please hurry. He did replace the pump and the building started warming up.

Two days later, we were receiving calls that it was cold in the building again. I immediately went to the boiler room and noticed that everything was performing normally. I was shaking my head when I exited the boiler room when I heard this weird noise as if there was a waterfall happening in our crawlspace under Jay's apartment. I opened the door and discovered large amounts of water cascading through Jay's apartment floor. Remember – Jay was in jail and nobody had been in that apartment for a month.

I ran as fast as I could to Jay's apartment. I opened the door to find the entire apartment was flooded. There was water gushing from a floor heat register in the living room and in the bedroom. I ran downstairs and shut the circulating pump down.

Apparently, when the pump was down the first time, Jay's pipes froze up. He had a corner apartment and all of his pipes on the outside walls froze. When the pump was replaced and turned on, it warmed the building enough to thaw Jay's pipes. The copper pipes split and water was being pumped all over his floors. The water was being pumped for two days and buckled all of the floors. All of the carpet was destroyed and the vinyl tile floors were also destroyed. Everything that was on the floor was soaked.

We called Service Masters to rehab the apartment. We had to store all of Jay's things in PODS outside the building. It took three months to rehab the apartment. It was a nightmare as far as I was concerned and it was all due to his damn pills!

Issue: You have a full time job? Really?

During my travels in and out of apartments and townhouses, I had met a wide variety of tenants. I genuinely liked and respected most of them. One tenant that I really liked was Jamar. Jamar was a cool dude that was always willing to assist me with anything that had to do with his building. Jamar and his girlfriend (with their only child) had a two bedroom apartment. They kept it very clean and organized.

Jamar would also let me know about things happening around there that he felt management should know. He was kind of an informant.

One day I asked him where he was from. He replied "Chicago, brother." I asked him "south side?" He replied "you know it." I told him that I was glad they made it out of there unharmed. He said that it was dangerous and he had to get the family out of that environment. I said "you seem like a smart guy, why government housing?" He said that when they moved out of Chicago, they didn't have enough money to get an apartment. I told him that our local company that employs around 3500 people is hiring. He said that he already worked there. I asked "You have a full time job? Really? I see you around here all day." He said that he worked second shift and that he had been there for two years. I said that was cool. Good for him.

So I was curious if he was paying any rent. I went to the office and looked up his file. I found out that Jamar wasn't even on the lease. Just his girlfriend and child were on the lease and they were "zero" renters which meant they didn't pay rent and they received vouchers from the State for their power and light bills.

I was torn what to do. Do I expose their fraud or just leave it alone? I got my calculator out and began to calculate how much money they had defrauded our government – us taxpayers to be exact. I took the rate of pay of $18 per hour times 40 hours a week – not counting overtime—which came to $720 per week minus taxes, insurance etc which was roughly 30 %. His take home pay was around $500 per week at least. When you're in government housing, the rent was 30% of your take home pay. So Jamar brought home around $2000 a month times 30% for rent. He should have been paying $600 a month towards rent. That's $7200 a year. Jamar had been working there over two years – that would equate to at least $14,400 he had defrauded the American taxpayers out of. Not only that, when his girlfriend filed her taxes, she received a $1,500 child tax credit. Now think about this – she didn't pay taxes at all; however, she received a check from the IRS of $1500.

There had been many times around the compound when I was doing routine maintenance requests when I would notice a new TV or new furniture and I knew the tenants were not working. When I'd say "Hey, that's a nice TV you have. When did you get that?" They would usually tell me that they got the TV with their tax return. They'd say "I got that with my refund!" I'd then say "I didn't know you were working." They'd usually say they weren't working. Then I'd say "well if you didn't pay anything in, how was it a refund?" They'd just look at me as if I didn't know what I was talking about. I'd leave it alone at that and have to chuckle.

Issue: He stole my kids toys

I was in my office one day when we received a call from the police that we needed to meet them at townhouse #9, building #6. My first thought was domestic abuse. The tenant had problems in the past with her baby daddy concerning custody and child support. The tenant (Melissa) lived in a townhouse with her ten-year-old son. When I first started this job, I was astonished at how filthy, dirty, and greasy Melissa's townhouse was. The whole apartment was like walking through an episode of Hoarders on the A&E channel. It was disgusting. It was obvious to me that Melissa needed some kind of intervention.

At first I would encourage her to do some cleaning. I tried to persuade her that if HUD did an inspection that they would force her to clean up the entire apartment – which was not true actually. HUD didn't care how filthy the apartment was. Their primary concern was safety issues. Nevertheless, I failed to get her off her butt and clean the place not just for herself but for her son as well. Melissa's kitchen and dining room walls were covered with grease, food and almost every stain you could imagine. I asked her to wipe the walls down and offered to paint them. She did try to wipe the walls down but it was like a 5th grader did it. I ended up painting over the disgusting walls in an attempt to make the place a little more livable.

Now back to the police call. We were summoned to the townhouse with a request for us to meet an officer there. I jumped into my field vehicle and drove over there to see what was going on. On the front patio area was an officer and Melissa. Melissa was pointing her finger at me yelling to the officer. I approached the two when Melissa started screaming at me for entering her apartment and stealing some of her kids toys. My immediate reaction was to laugh. After a good chuckle I said to Melissa "what the hell would I want with your kids toys?" She replied "some of his toys are missing and you have a key for the apartments! It was you! I just know it!" I replied "how dare you accuse me of that! I think you're fucking crazy!" I usually didn't swear or yell back however, she needed to hear that. Everyone around here coddled her from what I noticed and I was not going to do the same.

The police officer pulled me aside and apologized for calling me to her apartment but explained that they had to follow up on these calls – especially at, in her words, "these housing projects." I got back on my vehicle laughing and said to Melissa "get some help!" I returned to the office to report this stupid crazy complaint to Karen. We had a good laugh.

Issue: Shouldn't you boys be in school?

While conducting an inspection for our upcoming REAC inspection, I was at building #5, townhouse #9 pounding on the front door to begin the inspection. Nobody was answering. We posted the door the day before which meant we had the right to enter. I let myself in. The place was trashed. It was just plain filthy. The tenant (Connie) had two children – a boy in his early teens and a girl around nine years of age. Connie worked at the local drive in restaurant. I gave her credit for working; however, her place was nasty! I was hoping she would never move because if she did, we would have to replace all of the carpeting and some of the kitchen flooring. We would have to fix holes in the walls, paint virtually everything, scrub all of the appliances and I wouldn't even want to mention what we'd need to do in both bathrooms.

I noticed there was music coming from the basement. I went to open the basement door and found it missing. When I got to the basement, I discovered her son and his friend. I could tell right away they were smoking pot. I looked at them with disgust and asked "shouldn't you boys be in school?"

They looked at each other and started laughing. They told me that their moms didn't really care if they went to school or not. I asked them if the school cared. They said that their moms call in for them anytime they wanted. I was shaking my head in amazement thinking what kind of message their mothers were sending.

I conducted my inspection and had quite a list of things to repair. I then returned to the office and told Karen what I saw and how disgusted I was and that I would hate the day Connie moved out. Karen then started laughing. I said "what?" She said that Connie had given her notice to move yesterday – still laughing. I yelled "nooooooo!" After Karen stopped laughing, I asked her where in the hell she was moving to? She relied that Connie had applied for a HUD single family house and was approved. To which I replied, "so let me get this straight. Connie, who allowed her kids to destroy an apartment, allowed her pot-smoking teenager to stay home anytime he wanted to from school, kept a nasty, dirty, greasy townhouse was awarded a government single family home practically free? Are you fucking kidding me? What? A townhouse wasn't good enough for her?" Karen replied still laughing at me, "welcome to the dynamics of government housing."

Issue: Wow! That's a really nice car!

I was on a maintenance request in building #6 townhouse #8 when I noticed the tenant drive up in his new car. It was a full sized SUV that looked brand new. He entered the townhouse and I immediately said "wow! that's a really nice car!" He replied "thanks" and went upstairs.

I was thinking about how he and his wife could afford a car like that? I completed the maintenance request and immediately went to the office to talk to Karen. I told her that #8 just bought a really nice car and that I knew researching their file that neither of them worked. I asked Karen how that was possible. She said that our company was investigating them because somebody turned them in claiming that they had been working and not reporting their income for longer than two years. I exclaimed "that's fraud!" Karen replied, "I know. They are going to be evicted." I said "Evicted? They should be prosecuted! That's fraud!" Karen said she was going to give them a 30-day notice to vacate and if they left without being evicted, HUD would drop the case. I said "What? How much do you figure that they owed?" She replied "around $23,000." I left the office shaking my head again. It seemed every day I was shaking my head. I was thinking if someone went to Wal Mart and put something in their pocket and tried to leave without paying, the police would be called and they would be arrested -- but you could defraud the taxpayers out of $23,000 with ZERO consequences!

Issue: Free rent, free food, free electricity, a free phone and now free attorneys?

I was at my desk placing a supply order for upcoming repairs when a police officer came in to inform Karen that they conducted a drug bust in building #4 townhouse #1. They informed her that the tenant, Latreece, was ticketed for possession of a controlled substance last night at her townhouse. The police usually informed us of any drug related incidences that happened on the property.

Karen thanked them for the information. After the police had left the office, Karen asked me if I had seen anything nefarious going on at Latreece's place. I told her that I had noticed a couple of guys coming and going from her place in the last couple of months. I also noted that it wasn't unusual around the compound to see that. She said "yeah I know." She told me to keep an eye on the townhouse and that she was going to start the eviction process on her. I noticed a definite scowl on Karen's face. Karen hated having to go to court. She said it was unnerving.

103

Karen started the eviction process which included: obtaining the police report, filing the papers with the courthouse which cost $94.50 and hiring a third person at a cost of $50 to serve the tenant the summons. Then a court date would be set --- usually 3 to 4 weeks out.

The tenant and the representative of the company (in these cases Karen) had to show up to the courthouse on the predetermined date set by the courts. The judge typically read the case and rendered a verdict to evict or dismiss the case. It was pretty simple in our cases. If the tenant was found guilty of possession of a controlled substance, they had violated the lease and HUD rules and eviction ensued.

On the day of the eviction, Karen seemed agitated and on her way out the door. However, I wished Karen good luck. Two hours later Karen returned from court yelling as she entered the office door "I can't fucking believe it! That bitch went out and got a free lawyer through the state to fight her eviction!" I asked her what happened. Karen said that Latreece called the State to get a free lawyer to fight the eviction. I asked how could she do that? The lease clearly stated that if there were drug charges, they would be evicted and HUD backed us up. Karen said that the lawyer found a loophole in the papers I filed and the dumbass judge threw the case out and now she had to re-file. I asked what the loophole was. She said that when our company bought the complex they never legally changed the name of the complex and that even though the name on all of our paperwork said our name, we had to file under the previous name operating at our current name.

I said "wait a minute. You mean to tell me Latreece gets free rent, free food, free electricity, a free phone and now free attorneys?" She replied, "Yup!" I said "That's just fucking wrong. She abuses the system and free lawyer gets her off? I can't believe it." Karen replied "well believe it. Taxpayer lawyers protecting the guilty!" Karen added, "Don't worry. I am going to re-file and this time her free lawyer can't get her off." Note: Another $94.50 and $50 cost.

Issue: Oh my God! Something bad is going on over there!

I had just returned from one of our out-of-town sister complexes and entered the office hoping to sit down and finish some paperwork when I looked out our office window and noticed a guy holding a small child draped over both of his arms. The child appeared to me as lifeless. The guy had a very distressed look on his face. It looked as if he was searching for help and didn't know where to turn. I yelled to the office staff "Oh my God! Something bad is going on over there!" Right after that came out of my mouth, we heard sirens. I ran outside and was on my way to see what was wrong when I noticed an ambulance pull up next to the townhouse the guy came out of. The guy gave the child to the paramedics and ran inside the townhouse. There seemed to be a lot of confusion. There were three women that came out of the house and the guy that was carrying the child came out also. The three women were in hysterics. The guy was just walking around aimlessly. We then noticed that the paramedics put two young children in the ambulance and sped off with their sirens blaring.

The police showed up and took the guy into custody and conducted an impromptu investigation. After about 90 minutes, the police left with the guy in the back seat. We were all wondering what the hell happened.

The following day I came into the office and Karen asked me if I had seen the news last night. I said that I didn't. I had a foreboding feeling about what she was going to tell me. Karen said that Breelyn, the tenant in the townhouse that the ambulance had responded to, came into the office to explain what happened. Karen told me that Breelyn had some guests over there yesterday. Breelyn said it was her friend from Chicago with her 18-month-old twin boys and her friend's boyfriend. Breelyn said they were visiting for a few days.

I said ok, that explains the two young kids I saw go into the ambulance. So I asked what happened. Karen said that this girl's new boyfriend of three months was sick of his girlfriend's 18-month-old twin boys crying and fussing all day that he decided to step with all of his weight on their chests! I said "You're fucking kidding me! Are they ok?" She replied "He killed one. Probably the one you saw and the other one went on Flight for Life." She said that the police let the guy go after questioning him then decided that they made a mistake and are now actively searching for him.

The police eventually found him in Chicago and charged him with homicide. He was subsequently found guilty and sent to prison.

CHAPTER 10

Trying hard to understand

This chapter is dedicated to situations, issues, observations and an overall review of the everyday happenings that I experienced in the five years that I was a Regional Maintenance Technician.

Everyday was an adventure for me. I was searching for answers concerning the actions of the people who ended up in government housing. My questions included, but were not limited to – who were they? Where did they come from? How did they end up in government housing? How did the cultural differences impact their character – good, bad, indifferent? How could I make a positive difference to aid in the development of the nuclear and extended families that my team and I interacted with on a daily basis?

Part of our mission statement was that all of us in the company genuinely cared about the tenants and how we could assist them. Everyday, however, I witnessed things that left me shaking my head. And in trying hard to understand, I decided to use this chapter to present to my readers the things I dealt with on a daily basis and allow the readers to decide what behavioral patterns they felt were normal or outside that normal realm.

I grew up in a town with a population of 65,000 in the heartland of the United States and developed an understanding of the region's social issues and values. I learned through my surroundings growing up what I could count on through my life as normal behavior. As stated in the beginning of this book, it was instilled in me that life was a gift but not always easy. I was taught the differences between empathy and sympathy and how to respect all walks of life. This chapter is a compilation of my observations through the years with an objective look at the facts that might have you "trying hard to understand."

Fact: In most cases, we were not allowed to charge tenants for damages they caused in their townhouses/apartments. We were instructed not to charge them due to the "bottom line." The company understood that if we started charging tenants for damages that the majority could not pay for them. That would incur a lease violation and we would have to evict them and it would cost more to do that than just fixing the damages. Also, the years of damages that accumulated that remain unpaid would show up on the company's bottom line as debt. This would not be an acceptable issue. Here were some examples of damages --- carpet severely stained or ripped, vinyl flooring destroyed, window blinds, patio blinds, holes in walls, broken windows, broken doors, etc. We were instructed to fix the damages and move on.

Fact: I have had many tenants demand new everything in their townhouses/apartments. They demanded new stoves, refrigerators, carpeting, blinds etc. I was really surprised at this when I first started. I was thinking that these requests were unreasonable. In most cases, there was nothing wrong with the condition of the things in their homes. I was also thinking that they were not paying any rent and in my opinion, should be thankful. They would say things like this to me: "I don't like the color of the carpet" and "I don't like that kind of stove, can we replace it?" I would reply sometimes "this isn't Trump Tower" laughing. They usually would laugh with me. I had to explain that this was Federal Housing and there was limited money for those kinds of upgrades.

Fact: One complaint that I would bring into the office on almost a daily basis was screens and blinds. I found out early in my tenure that in family housing, the kids always seemed to ruin the screens in the windows and patio doors. I was always repairing them. I would always repair them and threaten to charge them the next time, even though we couldn't. This seems trivial, however, it happened so often and we were not allowed to charge them so it became quite trying for us maintenance people. Also, we had to build our own screens to fit the windows due to people breaking into the windows. It happened often.

Fact: Abandoned cars is a huge problem in the parking lots. At any given time there were at least 5 or 6 abandoned cars in the 3 parking lots on the compound. I would make an effort to find out who owned these cars and ask them to remove them. These cars usually had broken windows, flat or slashed tires, towels or sheets covering the windows etc. They made the place look like Harlem back in the 60's. We would threaten them that the vehicle would be towed and they would have to pay the towing fee to retain possession. The problem was that the company would have to pay the initial towing fee to have the car removed and be reimbursed when the owner paid the towing company to retain his/her car. The biggest part of this problem was that these cars were abandoned and the owners didn't want them back. Now the company was stuck with the towing bill. We were told that there was no budget listed for towing and to try to persuade the tenant to move the vehicle. They never did. We had abandoned cars all over the parking lots. It was quite frustrating to me because I wanted the property to look clean and appear that we cared --- because we did care.

Fact: Every day I came to work, the first thing I would do is get my field vehicle and pick up all of the garbage that was thrown all over the grounds the day before. You would think it was probably the kids throwing their candy wrappers and empty water bottles all over the place --- nope! It was everyone! The moms, dads, relatives, guests, kids, kids' friends, etc. It was extremely frustrating especially when there were garbage cans for them to use all over the grounds. Also, they would use the basement window area as garbage cans. Here is a small list of things I picked up daily: soda cans, water bottles, freezer pop wrappers, condoms, cigarette lighters, every kind of candy wrapper you could think of, empty bottles of expensive booze and beer, fast food bags and cups, broken toys and bikes. And that's the short list! If you thought about how much taxpayer money could be saved if everybody respected the "no littering" signs it would amaze you. Let's calculate. The company could save at least 6 hours a week at $16/hour – that would be around $100/week at 52 weeks a year. That would equate to $5200/year that the taxpayer paid to these projects. There are thousands of these projects around the country. It's easy to surmise that could cost taxpayers millions just to pick up garbage on the ground!

Fact: Dumpster areas were another problem for the maintenance departments. It was not unusual to come into work and find bags and bags of garbage surrounding the dumpsters. I learned early on to leave the dumpster covers open. I learned if I didn't, they would not be willing to simply lift up the cover to throw the garbage bag in the dumpster. Even when I left the covers open, many times they would still leave the bag in front of the dumpster. I also noticed that they would leave the bags on the grounds on their way to the dumpster. I wanted to open the bags to look for any mail inside. This mail would tell me what townhouse or apartment the trash came from. I would take the bag to the address and scold them for leaving the bag in the middle of the field. At first they would deny that it was their bag until I showed them their mail. Busted! Then they would blame it on their kids. I found it quite astonishing that they would force their young kids to take the garbage to the dumpster. I figured out that the kids couldn't reach the dumpster to throw the bag in and that's one reason for the garbage bags all over the place.

Fact: February and March were a bad time for the dumpster areas. Those months we noticed a huge influx of old dirty furniture, TV's, etc all around the dumpster areas. Those two months were the top two months for tax returns. They received around $1500 tax credit for each child in the household. However, in earlier chapters, I described that most didn't pay any taxes in because they were unemployed but yet still received a "TAX CREDIT?????" Well.... they would buy lots of new stuff with that money – creating a mess in the dumpster areas. They assumed that just because it was a dumpster area, they could take their old furniture and crap to be picked up by somebody free of charge!

Fact: When somebody applied and was accepted to Government Housing, most of the time it meant that they could keep that townhouse/apartment for life. This was the case of a tenant that was living in a three- bedroom townhouse alone. When I first started, I met Carol while performing a maintenance request. She was living in the townhouse by herself. I asked her how long she had been living there. She said she had been there almost 28 years. I asked her why a three bedroom? She said that she had two kids but they grew up and moved out 20 years ago. I asked her if she had a job. She said she hadn't worked since she moved there. She explained that after her divorce, she moved here with her two kids and had not worked since. She also said that her ex-husband skipped out on child support. She told me that she was awarded this townhouse and was told that she could live there for the rest of her life if she wanted to. Carol was a very nice person that kept her townhouse very clean. She didn't ever cause trouble and on occasion would let us know when she saw bad things going on there. My question was why hadn't she been asked to move to a one bedroom apartment where it would save taxpayer money. If Carol would win the lottery and want to pay back all of the free rent she received, she would owe 28 years of rent at approximately $600/month which would equal over $200,000. Carol was about 70 years old now. If she lived there for another 10 years at $750/month (market value) that would add another $90,000 onto the $200,000.

That didn't even county the electric company's voucher she received at $40/month --- which would add another $18,200. If we added on food stamps at $300/month it would add on another $136,000 if she was there another 10 years. The total cost to taxpayers for Carol was around $534,240.00.

Fact: Bed bugs had become a major problem within our properties. I found out that the problem didn't come from the tenants; however, it came from their guests. In talking with the tenants, we found out that they had many visitors from Milwaukee and Chicago – the capital of bed bugs, notwithstanding New York City. We experienced this issue so often that we were sent to a bed bug seminar. We were taught how to inspect and identify bed bugs. Once we identified that the house had bed bugs, we were required to call a professional extermination company. This whole process would get complicated. The tenant was required to get everything off of the floor and off of the furniture including beds. They were required to remove all light switch and outlet covers. There were a few more things they were required to do however, they never did it. This made it hard for the exterminator to perform their treatments. Usually, the exterminator had to return for treatments 3 to 4 times. This process was very expensive to the taxpayer. Remember, most tenants didn't pay any rent and that the taxpayer subsidized most of the costs of the entire complex which included pest removal. Note: I felt bad for the children's experiences with bed bugs. I did whatever I could to aid in the process.

Fact: There were many times that tenants would come into the office yelling and screaming at the office staff. They would threaten them on a regular basis. They seemed to lose control of their emotions so easily and fast. Many times Karen would have to threaten to call the police on them if they didn't calm down and talk rationally. Here were some examples of subject matter discussed:

On occasion a tenant would come in and demand that their locks on their doors be changed. When asked why, there was a plethora of reasons: I lost them. I don't want my baby daddy coming in anymore. My kids lost them etc. We knew that most times the baby daddy (who wasn't even supposed to be living there), had a key and the tenant didn't want him sneaking in. Anyways, when Karen told them that it was a $35 charge to change the locks, they typically went ballistic! They'd start questioning the cost yelling "why? That's a rip off!" when it was their fault to start with.

Another example. When we'd find out that the tenant was working and Karen would inform them that they'd have to start paying 30% of their income for rent, an argument would ensue.

I didn't even want to be on the property when they'd be informed they'd be evicted. They would even scream at the office staff when they'd come in to file a complaint on a friend or neighbor. Sometimes the tenants could be quite intimidating.

Fact: One issue that I found hard to understand was all of the food programs the State and local governments offered. One thing that I had noticed through the years was the overabundance of food that was packed in the cupboards and refrigerators of the tenants' homes. I started to notice this with some of our first "midnight movers." These tenants moved out without telling the office – typically sometime during the night. They'd take their clothes, TV's and sometimes their beds and leave everything else including food. I was amazed to find so much food left behind. The refrigerator/freezers and cupboards were packed with so much food that we would pack it up and take it to our community food bank for donation. Karen told me that the food stamp program was to blame. She said that most families here were awarded food stamp money on a monthly basis and in most cases, it was more than they could consume. She said that the school system around our town also supplied free lunches to 48 percent of the kids attending -- 48 percent!!! I commented that it didn't make sense that their homes were full of food and they still got free lunches provided by us taxpayers. Karen replied "I think it's because they are too lazy to prepare a lunch in the mornings and it's free anyway so why take the time." I noted to Karen that our local Advocap brought bag lunches to the complex during the summer once a week for everybody including adults and maybe they should know the truth about their packed shelves. Karen replied "you'd be wasting your time." I agreed with her but added "at least we wouldn't have to pick up all of the bag lunches thrown on the grounds."

Fact: When I first started, I noticed that our properties didn't have surveillance. I was amazed and concerned for the safety of the staff and the tenants. I asked Karen why we didn't have surveillance on the grounds and in the common areas. She said that she was surprised also and was petitioning the company to invest in them. After begging the company for over two years, they finally asked us to get them some quotes. We obtained quotes from 3 separate companies and submitted them. We were granted a contract to have a system installed. Now you are probably thinking that this was standard and why even add this to this book. Well…. here's the kicker to the issue – once the tenants found out that we were installing surveillance, we experienced a slew of families packing up and moving out of town. Apparently talking with the tenants who stayed, we found out that many of the people living there were either living there illegally or the police were looking for them. We lost around 12 families and more were considering leaving. Here we were, 12 empty townhouses and apartments abandoned in less than a week. Now I had to rehab 12 places, most of them full of abandoned furniture, food, clothes, beds, etc immediately. I called it the "SHIT STORM!" On a positive note: I knew in the long run that it was the right thing to do. I knew we would procure better tenants that were not concerned with the surveillance.

Fact: That last fact reminded me of this next quick fact. I had been there for about one year and I was always amazed at all of the phones calls we were getting every day. It seemed as if the phone would not stop ringing. I finally asked the office staff why the phone never stopped ringing? They told me that the majority of the calls were from people looking to apply for a townhouse or apartment. I asked from where? They said mostly Milwaukee and Chicago people looking to relocate. I remember the phone just ringing off of the hook. Until one day I came into work and Karen asked us for a staff meeting. We all went into her office and she told us that the police M.E.G unit contacted her last night and said that they were performing undercover surveillance for the past 4 months and there was going to be a huge bust today. She wanted us to be aware of the strange activity we might witness. The police raided 4 to 5 places and took a few people into custody. The word got out to all tenants that there was a huge bust and that there would be undercover agents all over the complex. Well it didn't take long for that information to reach Milwaukee and Chicago about the bust. It only took about a week and the phones started calming down. We estimated that we went from approximately 20 to30 calls a day to under 4 a day inquiring about housing. I found the situation to be quite astonishing.

Fact: In trying to understand Government Housing and how it worked and survived and where taxpayer money went, I found some aspects to be quite eye opening. One of the most eye opening experiences as a maintenance technician was when I was required to attend the company's national convention. I really didn't want to go. I knew that the convention was primarily designed for the regional property managers, property managers, office staff and service directors. I was required to attend the three day even which included daily seminars, a wide variety of expensive entertainment, free food morning, noon and a rather lavish dinner at night. My air travel was paid and also my lodging. When I arrived, I was bussed from the airport to the hotel to register and drop off my luggage. Then we were all bussed to the local zoo where we were treated with an animal show, a big band performance and a huge beautiful buffet.

After the activities, we were bussed back to the hotel for the evening. We woke up to a beautiful breakfast buffet and then were required to attend some classes, which I skipped out of because they had nothing to do with maintenance. After morning classes, we attended another beautiful buffet for lunch. We were required to attend a couple more classes, which I didn't, before the awesome sit down dinner which included key note speakers, motivational speakers followed by big name entertainment --- all paid for by the company. Sound great? The entire time I was there all I could do was think about the total cost of this outing to the taxpayers. Remember, this is a non-profit company providing affordable housing to thousands of families. I estimated using my experiences in other businesses that I worked for that the convention cost in excess of a half million dollars. There were over 400 people that attended. Took 400 times the cost of the food, travel, and hotel rooms which were private. Here is what it cost my company to send me: $300 for air travel, $150 for food, $350 for lodging. These costs alone totaled $800. Take $800 times 400 people which totaled $320,000. Now add to the $320,000 the cost of the entertainment, motivational speakers, convention center rental fee, bus travel etc. which I could confidentially say came to over a half million dollars for a 3 day event. I believed this was a total waste of taxpayer money.

Fact: One thing I found astonishing was that a lot of our tenants that didn't have any income as stated on their lease applications, had many personal items that didn't coincide with their zero income claims. I noticed that a majority of them had cars, newer TV's, I phones, cable tv, air conditioners, nice furniture, computers, etc. I was glad they had those things but wondered where they got the money to purchase them if they claimed that they had zero income. It didn't make sense to me.

Fact: One of the biggest problems that Government Housing experienced was the invited and uninvited people that actually lived on the properties illegally. To cite an example --- at our 88-unit complex we had at least 75 percent of units housing people who were not on the lease. The most common scenario was that the mom and kids applied for Government Housing and were awarded an apartment or townhouse. There had been many times when I was conducting a move-in where the mom and kids that were approved were with a gentleman also checking out the premises. I knew the gentlemen didn't drive up from Milwaukee or Chicago just to "see" the place. They came up here to live and hopefully have a safer and better life. Once the lease was signed and they moved in, there was virtually nothing we could do. Also, not just the dads but the brothers, sisters, uncles, aunts, cousins, friends, their friend's friends etc moved in sometimes for a month or much longer. I was instructed by management to give move-ins some time and wait until they started receiving mail. When that occurred, I had to take a photo of the mail when was conducting a maintenance call to prove that someone was living there that shouldn't be. I never did this because I genuinely felt sympathy for them. I knew most of these people came from hard backgrounds and felt that everybody deserved a chance to be a good citizen. If they had run-ins with the law, they were on their own and I let the justice system run its course. Too many times that was what happened.

Fact: I was very surprised when I began this journey as a maintenance technician who was responsible for the condition of every home, that almost every townhouse/apartment that I went into had a light cream colored carpeting. I was amazed at the condition in the places. The carpets were riddled with stains of every color. From red to purple to black, greasy stains and wear patterns were in almost every apartment I went into. I wanted to know who approved this color of carpeting. In a conversation with Karen, our property manager, she informed me that our corporate office had secured a corporate account with Sherwin Williams nationwide to have the same style and color carpet in every unit across the United States. As a landlord myself, I understood the need for conformity and standards as a company; however, my question was "why in family housing were we required to install light cream colored carpet?" Our company had many complexes all around the country and 90% of the were senior living facilities. I understood the thought process concerning senior living apartments ---- but not family housing. I decided to take the initiative to call our local Sherwin Williams store and change the color and style. I decided to start ordering very dark brown carpet in color with a very tight Berber style. This would mask most of the stains and made it much easier to clean. I started installing this type of carpet into the empty apartments as we refurbished them preparing for new move ins. The current tenants started talking to one another about the new style and they all wanted us to replace their existing carpet. I had to inform them that it wasn't in the budget but I would see what I could do sometime down the line. About two years and 40 townhouses/apartments later, I was called into Karen's office. She informed me that corporate discovered that I was deviating from their standards and to start ordering the designated color and style carpet. This upset me. I asked Karen who made the decisions on carpet. She replied 'someone at corporate.' I demanded that person's email. I said "whoever is making that decision obviously never walked through any of our family housing units." I drafted an email stating that they needed to reconsider their decision on family housing carpet standards and incorporate a new policy of the carpet the tenants were begging for. I also demanded an explanation why a light colored carpet? I added that it didn't make sense. Two weeks later, Karen received an answer. The geniuses at corporate said that, wait for this one...." we want a nice cream colored carpet so it doesn't appear to look like Government housing." I replied "WHAT!!!" I told Karen that's sending the wrong message! We **should** be encouraging our tenants that there are better things our there to strive for, not coddle them to become too comfortable in their current situations. I ignored corporate and called Sherwin Williams and demanded that they send the carpet I wanted --- not what corporate wanted and that I would take full responsibility. I prevailed! Note: I was not trying to disparage the company I worked for -- I had the utmost respect for the company and the housing complex, in general, helped many people.

Fact: One of the first days that I worked there I overheard Karen, the property manager, conducting a new lease signing with a family that took the bus from Chicago to our property. They were scheduled to sign the lease and move in that day. Karen was explaining to them all of the rules and regulations and mentioned that they needed $25.00 for a security deposit to move in even though they were zero renters. They didn't know they needed $25.00 and came up here with no money and just the shirts on their backs. They were scrambling to find $25.00. I was shocked on two fronts. One, I couldn't believe they came here with virtually nothing -- and two, that this mom didn't even have $25.00. I felt so bad for them. I offered to Karen that I would pay the $25.00 for them and she pulled me into my office and said "no, that's against company policy and it could cost you your job." I asked the new tenant if she knew anybody in town that could help her out. She said she did and that she would return. After an hour later, she found the money and we were able to get her into her new home. The fact remains is that it only cost $25.00 for a security deposit to move into a townhouse/apartment. If someone moved into an apartment that worked and had a job, then the security deposit was a little bit more. I found out why they never, and I mean never, cleaned their places when they moved. Would you clean carpets, bathtubs, sinks, kitchen/dining room floors, ceiling fans, windows, patio door glass, refrigerators, stoves, walls, toilets, etc, if your security deposit was only $25 to $100?

Fact: We had a call to the office from one of our tenants that her neighbor must have moved because she hadn't seen the mom of the kids in a long time. So we posted her door with a 24 hour right to enter. The following day, we entered to find most of her stuff was gone and no sign of anybody living there. The first thing I looked at was the expiration date of the milk container in the refrigerator. That usually told us how long they had been gone. The expiration date indicated that they had been gone for a half a year. I also looked at the toilets to see how much water was in the bowl. If the bowl was dry, that meant months. We tried to contact the tenant but we were unsuccessful. We checked with the electric company and the tenant stopped paying her bill a few months earlier. Usually the power company gave us a disconnection notice but they couldn't legally disconnect the power during the winter months. So the fact was that a tenant could move out without notice. This townhouse was vacant for 6 months while we taxpayers were fitting the bill. What concerned me was that another needy family could have had that home months ago.

CHAPTER 11

Why the wave of move-outs?

Toward the end of my tenure at my 88-unit complex where I was based out of and spent most of my time at, we had a wave of tenants moving out. It was a lot of move outs and all at once. We had many midnight movers and some that actually gave proper notice. I think I counted at least 15 townhouses/apartments empty or coming up empty. It was shocking to me and gave me the impetus to begin thinking about retiring. Our corporate office called us to find out what we were doing wrong to create this situation. I was taken aback by their accusation and quite frankly pissed off. I knew that we were extremely professional in our duties and directives. We treated everybody with the utmost respect and maintained a clean, safe place for families to live and thrive. I told Karen that I was the one in the field and that I was going to put a report on file as to why we were experiencing an unusual amount of move outs in such a short time. Here was a list of what I submitted to corporate. I produced a list of these reasons by townhouse/apartment without using the actual addresses. These things happened within a 2-month period which I called the "shit storm 2.0."

Townhouse: Moved due to domestic abuse
Townhouse: Moved due to baby daddy stalking
Apartment: Moved to a tax-deferred condo

Apartment:	Moved because was 3 months behind in rent of $136.00/month
Townhouse:	Evicted, in jail for drug dealing
Townhouse:	Harboring drug dealers, scared of them and midnight moved
Apartment:	Evicted, in jail for using hard drugs
Townhouse:	Moved to a 5 bedroom Advocap house
Townhouse:	Evicted, too many domestic abuse calls to the police
Townhouse:	Moved to a tax-deferred condo
Townhouse:	Moved due to neighbor's pot smoking
Townhouse:	Moved after her brother shot up an apartment
Apartment:	Moved because her baby daddy wasn't approved to move in

That was the information that I submitted to the company. And remember, that was about a **2-month period**. I also added that a relatively new construction company had been building a lot of tax-deferred condos that had garages and other attractive amenities. I had to assure corporate that this wave of move-outs was due to a menagerie of reasons. I also asked them to review their lease standards for acceptance. One of the areas that I wanted them to review was the eviction rule which stated if they had been evicted for any reason in the past 6 years, they'd be disqualified. My argument was that the tenants were looking for government housing because they were evicted. Also, the disorderly conduct rule needed to be revisited. If a prospective tenant was cited with a disorderly conduct charge within the last 6 years, they too should be disqualified from our units. I felt (given my experience) that we should allow people who have had trouble in the past a chance to move in. Everybody deserved a second chance to turn their lives around.

CHAPTER 12

Opinion piece by economist Walter Williams

One of my goals in this book was to document some behavioral social attitudes that I had witnessed. I wanted to explore what we could do to inform, teach, persuade, educate or just plain help some of our fellow Americans to realize and understand that some types of behavior was just not the norm. When I started in Government Housing, it took me about a year to realize why some people conducted their lives in the manner in which they do. My conclusion: "They felt that their actions were **just plain normal.**"

I came across an article written by economist Walter Williams. Mr. Williams is an American economist, commentator, and academic scholar as well as a syndicated columnist and author known for his classical, liberal and libertarian conservative views. I was struck by the article he wrote. I included this article to this book because it offered facts and insight pertaining to certain sectors of our society. In a way, I found this article helpful in explaining to all the players in the "system" that there were choices in life that could lead us down a path of self-respect and self-responsibility toward their future or down a path of self-deprivation and dependency. I found it crucial that we reach our young children early to reveal the realities of each path taken. I personal would love to have an opportunity to go directly to the source of this systemic problem we have been enduring as an evolving nation for 200 years and lecture to our young and vulnerable about the consequences of their actions.

Here is the article by Walter Williams, "America's problem is Dependency, not P overty"

There is no material poverty in the U.S. Here are a few facts about people whom the Census Bureau labels as poor.

Dr Robert Rector and Rachel Sheffield, in their study "Understanding Poverty in the United States" Surprising Facts About America's Poor" (http://tinyurl.com/448flj8) report that 80 percent of poor households have air conditioning, nearly three quarters have a car or truck and 31 percent have two or more. Two thirds have cable or satellite TV.

Half own one or more computers, while 42 percent own their homes. Poor American have more living space than the typical non-poor person in Sweden, France or the U.K. What we have in our nation are dependency and poverty of the spirit, with people making unwise choices and leading pathological lives aided and abetted by the welfare state.

The Census Bureau pegs the poverty rate among blacks at 35 percent and among whites at 13 percent. The illegitimacy rate among blacks is 72 percent and among whites is 30 percent. A statistic one doesn't hear much about is that the poverty rate among black married families has been in the single digits for more than two decades, currently at 8 percent. For married white families it's 5 percent.

Now the politically incorrect questions: Whose fault is it to have children without the benefit of marriage and risk a life of dependency? Do people have free will, or are they governed by instincts?

There may be some pinhead sociologists who blame the weak black family structure on racial discrimination. But why was the black illegitimacy rate only 14 percent in 1940, and why, as Dr. Thomas Sowell reports, do we find that census data "going back 100 years, when blacks were just one generation out of slavery... showed that a slightly percentage of blacks adults had married than white adults. This fact remained true in every census from 1890 to 1940"?

Is anyone willing to advance the argument that the reason the illegitimacy rate among blacks was lower and marriage rates higher in early periods was there was less racial discrimination and greater opportunity?

No one can blame a person if he starts out in life poor, because how one starts out is not his fault. if he stays poor, he is to blame because it's his fault. Avoiding long-term poverty is not rocket science. First, graduate from high school. Second, get married before you have children, and stay married. Third, work at any kind of job, even one if it starts out paying minimum wage. And finally, avoid in engaging in criminal behavior.

It turns out that a married couple, each earning minimum wage, would earn an annual combined income of $30,000. The Census Bureau poverty line for a family of two, is $15,500, and for a family of four, it's $23,000. By the way, no adult that starts out earning the minimum wage does for very long.

Since Lyndon Johnson declared war on poverty, the nation has spent about $18 trillion at the federal, state and local levels of government on programs justified by the "need" to deal with some aspect of poverty means you could purchase everything produced in our country each year and then some. There's very little guts in the political arena to address the basic causes of poverty. To do so risks being labeled as racist, sexists, uncaring and insensitive. That means today's dependency is likely to become permanent.

Printed in the United States
by Baker & Taylor Publisher Services